TRUE GRID

Discovering God's Custom-Designed Blueprint for You

By Charlynne M. Boddie

True Grid

Discovering God's Custom-Designed Blueprint for You

Managing Editor: Gayle Smart

Editor: Kay duPont
Proofreader: Rose Taylor
Book Designer: Paula Chance

True Grid Publishing

Library of Congress Number 2004092244

ISBN: 0-9753392-0-6

Printed in the United States of America

10 9 8 7 6 5 4 3 2 1

Dedication

For every princess or prince out there who is on their way to discovering God's master blueprint for their life. When you fall down on the journey, causing your crown to tilt and you scrape your knees, dust yourself off and keep on walking with your hand firmly planted in the loving grip of the Master Dream Maker and High King of Heaven — Jesus Christ.

Dear Alma—
Walk in His Divine
Greatness!
Charlynne M. Boddie
Ps 139:13-16

Acknowledgements

To Linda Evans Shepherd for believing in this book, giving me something to put in it of yours, and showing me how to write it. Your friendship and mentoring mean so much. This book wouldn't be without your guidance.

To Keith Harrell for introducing me to the folks at James & Brookfield and seeing something of substance in the project. God bless you for giving it and me a listen.

To my amazing girlfriends: Michele Hendry, Brenda Wheeler, and Liz Brown. When the going got tough, you not only prayed with and for me, but you gave me the use of your homes for writing and unwinding. Each of you are the best hostesses! I love you dearly.

To Faith O'Halloran for praying with me in the wee hours of the morning and always having something positive to say to me along the way. Your advice and prophetic timeliness is invaluable to me, today and always. Thank you for the gift of your time.

To Alistair Bullen and Robert Comstock for being two men of enormous vision who have deposited their spirit of faith that has fueled me for many years, making me believe that I really can do anything God says I can do. Both of you are businessmen of the highest excellence and I am proud to call you my friends.

To Peter DeAnello, my favorite motivational speaker. Your wisdom and humility are deep and wide.

To my Mom, Sandra Boddie, for setting the amazing Christian living example for me all the days of my life and for teaching me the importance of the parable of the talents in Matthew 25 and Luke 19 at age 11, setting the course for my dream life. God bless you, Mom, for choosing to raise me like you did and for all the sacrifices you made along the way!

To my sister and business partner, Shaunya Boddie, for believing in me even when I didn't always believe in myself. You are a master writer and a great source of inspiration to me and I love you!

To Jackie Jacobsen for being my friend and mentor. You have deposited a wealth of knowledge into me that I will carry througout the rest of my life. You have never stopped believing in the vision God had for my life...even in the darkest of times.

To my intimate allies: Aundrey Wilkins, Joy Morgan, Karla Sullivan, Fiona Vickers, Jill Mitchell, Donna Dyck, Bev and Andy Rowe, Helen Mahoney, Amanda Collins and Sharman and Brian Jeffries for your consistent and earnest prayers and advice to me over the years. I love you all for standing with me and holding me accountable to God's word in my life!

To these prophetic ministers: Freddy Halcomb, Dee Dee Thompson, Marilee Bruno, Marcia Hinds, Jean Randall, Tom Munger, Pastor and Mrs. Al Scott, Pastor Jan Painter, Stuart Bellamy, Jon Thatcher, Pastor Charlotte Cronk, Rev. Kathryn Towne, Lillian Blackman, Pastor Pat Mahoney, Pastor Gary Pack, Pastor Mary Lindow, Tim Storey, Rich and Gail Harris, Paul and Amanda Williams and Lelonnie Hibberd. Each of you has spoken a word into my life that has been pivotal to the fruition of my X-treme Dreams. Thank you for your obedience to the voice of the Holy Spirit. Those words are all part of God's master blueprint for me and are bearing much fruit in my life today!

To Neal Donop — You are one of my most favorite unsung heroes because of the wild call on your life and the strength of your quiet confidence. You have given so unselfishly to me and I am deeply moved by the fact that you would partner with me, all the way from Beijing, China! I thank God that you did because I wouldn't be watching this dream become a reality without you. Thank you for sharing your gifts with me and believing in this from day one. Glad you came along for the ride.

To Jesus, High King of Heaven and the Architect of my X-treme Dream — I am nothing without You. May I decrease that You might increase in my life. Thank you for allowing me to record and report what You are doing in so many lives around the world throught the True Grid process. You have my love and devotion forever.

Table of Contents

FOREWORD

I first met Charlynne in 1988 when she came to our church as part of a team from the States. What impressed me then was her extreme enthusiasm, determination and hunger for God. This shines through in these pages. It is great to teach when someone really picks up the ball and runs with it — with the vision grid and with this book, Charlynne has done just that. I applaud the practical nature of this book and the interactive elements for the reader, which makes it a more valuable learning tool.

Alistair Bullen, ABA Designs
Ascot, England.

Introduction

What would happen if everyone did something for his or her vision each day? I believe the world would be changed.

But can we find God's vision for our lives? I believe He never wanted it to be a mystery. My book, *True Grid*, will show the reader how to discover and how to unearth the gold nuggets in His Word. These treasures applied to a life will make dreams come true.

True Grid: God's Custom-Designed Blueprint for You is an exciting book that shows Christians how to tap into the original plan God designed for them before they were even born. This book gives people from every race, culture and socio-economic background simple, practical steps to live God's unique vision for them and see extraordinary, miraculous results. Christians reading this book will step into a deeper level of intimacy with their Creator and more meaningful relationships with people in the body of Christ. *True Grid* propels readers into an extreme adventure of the wildest kind that brings fulfillment and joy to their destinies. It's a paradigm shift of everything we've ever heard about vision and God's ability to make the impossible happen through the '*suddenlies*' of life.

Chapter 1

You are X-tremely Unique!

Each one of us is God's purpose wrapped in flesh and blood.
— Gary Pack

*Our deepest fear is that we are powerful beyond measure.
We ask ourselves, 'Who am I to be brilliant, gorgeous, talented and fabulous?' Actually, who are you not to be? You are a child of God.
We are born to make manifest the glory of God that is within us.*
— Marianne Williamson

Vision is a God-sized idea . . . a dream with wheels and a road map.
— George Barna

The privilege of a lifetime is being who you are.
— Joseph Campbell

On a clear night, you can see stars too infinite to count. Each one is different because God made it that way. And just as He has created an infinite number of stars in the heavens, so has He created within each human being the ability to dream and carry out a vision to its completion.

A single mother named Angela felt that she was one of those forgotten "stars" in God's big universe. She had a beautiful baby girl out of wedlock and was seen as a disgrace by her earthly father. It seemed that Angela had lost not only her dream, but her future to work in the entertainment industry as a director. How or why would God zero in on her miserable life to deliver her into all she could be?

Angela discovered that God does make dreams come true. She decided to listen to God speak to her through one of my X-treme dream personal seminars. After she learned how to dream with God, a series of doors opened up to her in less than two years that landed her the dream job she had prayed for! Now she is working as an assistant director for a top TV director overseas. Angela knows without doubt that God cares about every dream spoken and unspoken in her heart. God never forgot Angela and He hasn't forgotten you!

God is the ultimate visionary and He has had a specific vision in mind for each of us since before we were born. Nothing about your birth is an accident.

PSALM 139:13-16

For You created my inmost being; You knit me together in my mother's womb. I praise You because I am fearfully and wonderfully made; Your works are wonderful, I know that full well. My frame was not hidden from You when I was made in the secret place. When I was woven together in the depths of the earth, Your eyes saw my unformed body. All the days ordained for me were written in Your book before one of them came to be.

**All Scripture is from the* New International *or* Amplified Bible, *unless otherwise noted.*

So what do I mean by **vision**? *Webster's Dictionary* tells us that visions are ideas, schemes or plans considered impractical or impossible by others.

I personally believe vision is that special something inspired by God that keeps you awake at night. Vision is those thoughts that cause you to realize your fondest dreams and hopes and make them a reality. Vision is whatever burns deep down inside your heart of hearts. Vision is those purposes and plans God desired for you before you came out of your mother's womb. Yes, it's His original blueprint for you.

Hard to fathom? Well, it's no small wonder! We live in an age of advertising that encourages all of us to think alike, dress a certain way, drive certain cars, and live and love in certain ways. God has designed us to be uniquely magnificent in Him, the Ultimate Multifaceted One. We were each created in His image and there are infinite numbers of visions waiting to be discovered and lived out all over the earth.

God is all about diversity of vision. Just as no two stars are created the same, so it is with man. No two people can carry out a vision in exactly the same way. Each person brings something different to the table. No vision is better than another person's vision, just different.

With vision, we can soar to new heights in God. Without it, we perish. That is why Scripture admonishes us to keep the vision we have before us.

HABAKKUK 2:2-3

And the Lord answered me and said, Write the vision and engrave it so plainly upon tablets that everyone who passes by may [be able to] read [it easily and quickly] as he hastens by. For the vision is yet for an appointed time and it hastens to the end [fulfillment]; it will not deceive or disappoint. Though it tarry, wait [earnestly] for it, because it will surely come; it will not be behindhand on its appointed day.

Today television brings us "extreme sports." Flip the switch and you can see athletes of all sorts doing wild, edgy things on surfboards, skis and skateboards. You assume that people who enjoy these types of activities are not your average, run-of-the-mill athletes. They are people who push the envelope in whatever sport they choose.

The God we serve is also like that. He has created a supernatural thing called the **X-treme dream**. What is the X-treme dream? It is all you would achieve if you knew you had no way of failing. **The X-treme dream is the balance between carrying out the vision God custom-designed for you and handling your heart's burdens and daily responsibilities**. For we know that all things are possible to those who believe.

MARK 9:23

If you can believe, said Jesus, everything is possible for him who believes.

I can remember thinking as a little girl how much fun it would be to live like a real princess. "Cinderella" was one of my favorite stories. The focus for me wasn't on the tangible things the heroine gained by marrying Prince Charming and moving up to his castle. My thoughts hung on the way Cinderella believed.

The closest I could get to experiencing Cinderella's transformation was my "coming out" ball as a 16-year-old debutante. This special event was a time-honored tradition in my family. I can remember staring at my mother's picture of her debutante ball in Miami, Florida. Her elegant dress was very much like Cinderella's, complete with long, white gloves. As I touched the glass in the photo, I knew I wanted to be just like her someday. I wanted to be presented to society as a lady.

When I turned sixteen, the Lord caused my dream to come true! Mom and I picked out my white, sparkly ball gown, complete with the long, white gloves. It was truly an evening of bliss as I walked down the staircase and met my date on the ballroom floor to begin the waltz. I will never forget it as long as I live! But instead of a white coach with beautiful horses, God arranged for me to be driven to the ball in a sleek, black limousine, ordered just for me. See, God knows exactly what is needed for every person's dreams, no matter where you are in your life.

Stop for a minute and see if you can remember the last time you had the kind of faith to believe that something unimaginable was possible. Are you hard-pressed to remember something like that? If so, you are certainly not alone. Many people in today's world have given up on thinking about any sort of "fairy tale" of their own. In fact, they have lost their God-given ability to dream anything.

The enemy of our souls is a dream stealer. His name is Lucifer and he wants you to believe that where you are right now is all you will ever be. Lucifer is the father of lies, and if we believe his press we have bought at least one of his lies. Do you ever feel guilty for believing you can be a part of God's manifested glory? If you said yes, then the X-treme dreams God has planned for you since before you were born have been buried in your heart. You have effectively banished your dreams to Never-Never Land. Today you believe those dreams are dead and gone forever. This belief could not be farther from the truth!

I want you to know, dear reader, that you have all you need right now to live your very own fairy tale (2 Peter 1:3). When you give your heart to the King of the universe, it's a million times better than having a fairy godmother! Cinderella gave her heart to a mere mortal. Have you any idea how much you are worth to our King? Do you have any idea what you have inherited from Him? If you'd like to take a peek at some of the things the King of our hearts says about our inheritance, read on.

I CORINTHIANS 2:9-10

But on the contrary, as the Scripture says, What eye has not seen and ear has not heard and has not entered into the heart of man [all that] God has prepared (made and keeps ready) for those who love Him [who hold Him in affectionate reverence, promptly obeying Him and gratefully recognizing the benefits He has bestowed]. Yet to us God has unveiled and revealed them by and through His Spirit, for the [Holy] Spirit searches diligently, exploring and examining everything, even sounding the profound and bottomless things of God [the divine counsels and things hidden and beyond man's scrutiny].

When you believe in Christ Jesus and ask forgiveness of your sins, not only are you forgiven, but you instantly become a prince or princess of the Most High God. You are an heir with Christ of the Kingdom of Heaven. The Holy Spirit within us allows us to hear from the Lord what our special piece of that kingdom looks like. God has a unique adventure planned and mapped for each of us, but we must agree to take His hand and trust Him. Opening up that perfectly wrapped dream is what this book is all about. Only you can open up the X-treme dream He has for you.

I learned this lesson as a scared, seventh-grade girl who found herself at a new school because her parents were going through a separation. My mom, sister and I had moved in with my cousins in Toledo, Ohio, and were attending an inner-city Catholic academy called St. Angela Hall. I was so discouraged with the way my life had turned out. On most days I just wanted the ground to open up and swallow me whole.

The nuns at St. Angela Hall knew about our situation and were very kind toward my sister Shaunya (Shonya) and I. Because we were both straight-A students, they paid special attention to how they could encourage our hearts during this very difficult time.

Soon after we enrolled, the nuns approached my mother about some special classes they offered for "gifted and talented" students. Mom agreed that we could both participate. There was a creative writing course and some other extracurricular options in the area of voice and speech. The writing class was fun and I enjoyed writing with my younger sister, but then they approached me about competing for state speech competitions. If I agreed to do it, I'd be coached by an elderly nun named Sister Mary Charles.

Since our move from our beloved Columbus, Indiana, my emotions had been as jiggly as the Jell-O on Bill Cosby's commercials. The small town of 44,000 I'd come from was its own sort of living fairy tale, founded by a group of Harvard men many years back. It was full of art, culture and a strong group of philanthropists. The town had also been featured in *National Geographic* several times for its world-class architecture. People hardly ever locked their doors in those days and crime was almost nonexistent. How I missed it. There was no comparison between my old life and my new.

Although I was the only black person in my class at St. Columba, my Catholic grade school in Columbus, I had never experienced prejudice of any kind. I had been at that school since I was five years old, and I sorely missed it.

My dreams there were shattered when my parents began to have trouble in their marriage. That's why we moved to Ohio.

Now I was living in a big city, going to a school where black students were the majority, and I was an outcast. The black students didn't like that I spoke perfect English, and they disliked even more the way studies came so easily for me. My new nickname became "Books and Homework." My peers hated me and, like the old Michael Jackson song, they wanted me to "go back to Indiana." I dreaded each day of school and had no desire to draw any attention to myself in any way.

Even though my mother was working diligently to finish a degree in psychology at Toledo University, as well as doing a practicum at a mental health institution, she took the time to chat with me about the opportunity to compete in speech competitions. She thought it was a marvelous idea and could not understand why I wasn't excited.

Remember how it was as a young teen? If something was going on at school that didn't thrill you, you often kept it to yourself. Ratting on someone was the absolute worst thing you could do, and so you didn't. So my mother did not have a clue about my school life. She didn't know that I was getting some pretty terrifying threats from my classmates at St. Angela Hall. Almost daily someone told me they wanted to cut off all my long, black hair or slice me up with a switchblade for not conforming to their ways.

Mother asked me to look with her at the parable of the talents (Matthew 25:14-30). We read it and then she went to study at the library. I was left alone to ponder these things in my own heart and make a decision.

I remember crying my eyes out that night because I felt the tug of the Holy Spirit telling me that everything was going to be all right but that I would need to take a leap of faith and say yes to the open door in front of me. Why me? Why couldn't someone else do it? Didn't He know I just wanted to go to school and avoid getting killed?

I had been tempted to play small and shrink so others wouldn't feel so insecure around me. What would happen if I didn't? Should I care what everyone else thought of me?

That night I heard the Lord say quietly to my heart that He wanted to do something special if I'd just trust Him and do the next thing. I felt He wanted me to say yes to Sister Mary Charles. The words of the Master to the faithful servants kept rolling around in my head. The two servants who multiplied what their master had given them reaped in abundance and were able to share in the master's joy.

MATTHEW 25:23

His master said to him, Well done, you upright [honorable, admirable] and faithful servant! You have been faithful and trustworthy over a little; I will put you in charge of much. Enter into and share the joy [the delight, the blessedness] which your master enjoys.

I decided to give Sister Mary Charles a chance as my speech coach. Every week I went into the dark, warm halls of the old Gothic-styled convent that was on the same campus as the academy. The halls led me to Sister Mary Charles, who had a real love for the dramatic arts and a knack for pulling things out of me that I didn't even know were there. She decided that I should enter the humorous poetry category for the statewide competition that year. Some 800 schools were sending students to compete.

On the day of the competition, my mom went with me and we carpooled with the nuns. I was a nervous wreck, but the Lord and I had made a pact. I would hold His hand and He would hold mine.

Soon it was my turn to present my humorous poetry. I didn't miss a word or stanza or go over the allotted time. When I was finished, I was one happy camper! At the end of the day, we went to the large assembly hall for the moment of truth.

When they called my name as the state winner for the humorous poetry category, I could hardly believe my ears! I had won a competition against 800 others. As I walked to the platform to receive my medal and ribbon, I heard the Lord speak to my heart: "There's more where that came from! Sit back and enjoy the ride!" As exciting as that was, I was happiest because I knew God had made good on His promise to me.

That was the highpoint of a very hard year. Even though my parents divorced, God didn't divorce me! Instead, He promised me the moon and more!

He promises you the same thing! It doesn't matter to Him what color you are, what denomination you are from, or how much money you do or don't have in the bank. You are His and He is yours.

The Lord wants us to act, walk and talk like we know we have the keys to His kingdom, because we do! The best fairytale in the world can't measure up to what He has for us. I don't ever want to end up like the servant who did nothing with the talents and abilities the Lord gave him. I want to give back to Him in a multiplied form what He's given to me.

We can go to "the ball" with Him anytime we like because we are already princes and princesses, and your journey to the ball can begin whenever you like. And guess what? You get to come as you are! There is no dress code where He is concerned. You are already perfect in His sight. He just wants you to come!

Would you like to make the King of the universe your dance partner forever and ever? Just put your hand in His. He has music for you to dance to that no one has ever heard before. The music is unique and for you alone. Why? Because you are X-tremely unique and there is no one else like you in the entire universe.

We've defined vision and the X-treme dream, but how do we define the things in life that can take our focus off God's vision for us? I place these things into two distinct categories:

The first is what I call **burdens of the heart**. These are our pet projects or hobbies that can get in the way of fulfilling a dream or vision. There is usually nothing wrong with these things in and of themselves, but they must be put into proper perspective. These burdens can have an emotional pull on us.

For example, say that you've always wanted to volunteer time to a community youth organization. That's certainly a worthy cause. The question is this, however: Is this concern a part of the overarching blueprint for your life or something you need to revisit from a different perspective? There is a place for this activity. It might just need to be weighed against your vision. You must ask the Lord how it fits into the picture.

The other category of things that can deter us from fulfilling the vision is **responsibilities**. We each have all sorts of day-to-day activities that we must do to pay the bills, take care of ourselves and our families, keep our jobs and handle problems. God knows we must live in this world, and at the same time He calls us to seek His kingdom first.

MATTHEW 6:31, 33

So do not worry, saying, What shall we eat? or What shall we drink? or What shall we wear? But seek first His kingdom and His righteousness, and all these things will be given to you as well.

As we take this X-treme dream journey together, I'll share with you how to balance your vision, your X-treme dream, your heart's burdens and your daily responsibilities. The Lord is just waiting for you to partner with Him and say *Yes*!

Chapter 2

Your X-treme Dream Journey Checklist

Whether or not I hear God's call depends upon the state of my ears; and what I hear depends upon my disposition.

— Oswald Chambers

What lies behind us and what lies before us are tiny matters compared to what lies within us.

— Ralph Waldo Emerson

I'm a firm believer in the theory that people only do their best at things they truly enjoy.

— Jack Nicklaus

Cherish your visions and your dreams, as they are the children of your soul — the blueprints of your ultimate achievements.

— James A. Froude

Your purpose is already inside you, and the following activities will help the parts of your vision rise to the surface. Allow yourself to **fully** seek the Lord's face for a clear understanding of your destiny. The checklist I am about to give you is vitally important to the success of your vision process.

1. Set aside a whole day or weekend just for you.

This is time just for you. See it as an investment in yourself. Be sure you will have no distractions or interruptions from the phone, fax, unexpected guests, children, pets, etc. Make this time a very special date with you and the Lord. Give yourself permission to do this.

2. Go someplace quiet.

Make sure this is a place where you can pray and really think about where you are at this time in your life. Do not be afraid of silence.

3. Allow yourself to travel back to when you were young.

Think about all that made you happy and what you loved being or doing. What things or places did you gravitate toward as a child? Did people notice certain traits or characteristics about you? What was one of your earliest and best dreams?

4. With colored pens, pencils, paint or crayons, write down whatever comes to mind.

God is so colorful when He creates. We are designed to be creative, too. Hold nothing back. Jot down words, phrases, pictures, places or people that come to mind.

5. Make your own treasure map from the jewels hidden deep in your heart.

Take a stack of old magazines and cut out anything and everything you see that pertains to your dreams, your vision and who you are. Look for places and people you connect with. Find phrases and words that tell who you are. If something leaps off a page at you, cut it out and paste it onto posterboard or into a sturdy blank book with lots of pages. Take your time with this exercise and go hog wild over this opportunity to explore and visualize exactly where you are at this time in your life and where you want to be.

6. If it helps to play music from your past, do it.

Music can take you back in time very quickly. Most of us can instantly remember exactly where we were and what we felt like at a certain time or place just by hearing a song. What memories from your youth or teen years are tied to specific songs? Maybe it's music from a favorite movie. If so, think about why you connect to the music and the movie. Jot those thoughts down.

7. Brainstorm as long as it takes you to exhaust every nook and cranny of your younger years.

Who were your friends and what were they like? Who were your favorite role models and why? What did you and your teachers discuss as you grew up?

Who made the deepest impression on you?

8. Take time to go through old photo albums of yourself, or even high school and college yearbooks.

Recapture the innocence and newness of those times. See if you can watch some old movies/videos of yourself.

9. Interview family members and friends.

Ask them what you were like as a child. Dig deep to find out others' impressions of you throughout your growing-up years. This is important. Remember that you are looking for clues to God's original blueprint for your life — the X-treme dream.

10. Take these pieces of information and begin to write down a full report of your findings.

Stay true to what you've rediscovered about yourself. The dream has always been there. You just needed time to go back to it and allow yourself to see it again.

None of the information needs to be in order right now. It's more important to get it written down so you have something to start with. The order will come later in the process of carrying out your X-treme dream.

Why is revisiting who and what we were like as children so important to the X-treme dream process? Children are pure and innocent. To them, anything is possible. As we mature into adulthood, we often lose the ability to dream and see visions the way children do. That's why God loves for each of us to retain "childlike faith."

LUKE 18:17

I tell you the truth; anyone who will not receive the kingdom of God like a little child will never enter it.

Know that checking off this list could take several days. But make yourself do it no matter what, and don't rush yourself. Examine carefully everything that comes to mind and all of the answers you find. There's no ticking clock like on "Wheel of Fortune." There is only the patient love of your Father who is there with you every step of the way. You are not in competition with anyone. You can rest in Him and the knowledge that you are in the palm of His hands and He has everything under control.

Once you have given yourself plenty of time to ponder these things you've rediscovered about yourself, you are ready to begin the rest of the quest. In the next chapter, we'll take a look at connecting God's order with the information you discovered. Keep your dancing shoes on. This is the part where you begin to see the Lord do some fancy footwork, with you as His beloved partner. He's going to sweep you off your feet!

CHAPTER 3

TRUE GRID: THE ANATOMY OF YOUR VISION

The path to long-range goals is paved with short-range objectives.
—ANONYMOUS

Obstacles are what you see when you take your eyes off the goal.
— ANONYMOUS

Do the thing you fear; and the death of fear is certain.
— RALPH WALDO EMERSON

If the dream is big enough; the facts don't count.
— PETER DEANELLO

A few years ago, one of my mentors, Alistair Bullen, called from his home in England to ask if I'd be interested in being one of the group session leaders for a gathering of businesspeople at a summer conference in England. One of the main topics to be discussed was vision. I jumped at the opportunity, not knowing how much that trip would change my life and the lives of others.

The tool presented to you in this chapter was first presented at that summer event, and I believe it's truly a gift from the mind of God. Those who have used it have become successful visionaries all over the world and are now living out their X-treme dreams. So if you'd like to join this fast-growing group, read the following story.

Sue and Ben had both been laid off from their jobs. They were coming to the X-treme dream seminar to gain some hope and see what could be done to right their circumstances. The situation was especially tough because theirs was a second marriage for both of them, making for a blended family. They were quite devastated by the recent events in their lives not to mention the needs of their six children. Could God really turn their messy situation around? How could they be expected to dream big when they were in the midst of a real crisis? Besides, isn't it a bit selfish to dust off your personal dreams when you have a rather large household to support?

Sue cried a great deal when I first asked her to share the dream in her heart of hearts. She had not finished high school and really wanted to become a writer on Christian women's issues, and perhaps even write a book someday. But in her mind this dream was next to impossible. She didn't have time to write and felt her dyslexia and lack of education was too big a barrier to cross.

Ben, on the other hand, confided in me that his deep desire was to take his great accounting skills to an extreme level on the international side of big business. But he had pushed his dream down so far that it hadn't seen the light of day in ages. He didn't see how an unknown accountant like himself could ever gain status and rank in a large international business.

After I congratulated the couple for having the courage to express their X-treme dreams, I shared with them the same tool you're about to discover.

I call it a Vision Grid. Sue and Ben used this tool and God moved mountains for them as a result.

By partnering with God and using the grid, Ben and Sue's dreams came true!

Ben went from being an unknown accountant to being the chief financial officer for a multimillion dollar corporation that brought several U.S. hotel chains to Europe for the first time ever! This was a promotion for him straight from God and it made room for Sue's dream to become a reality. Because of the extra cash flow in their home, Sue had the time and money to complete her education, go on to college, and write to her heart's content! She received a national honor as a writer within a short time, now she helps other women learn to write better and is working on a doctoral degree.

All of this happened in less than three years. The X-treme dream grid brought focus, abundance and God's divine order to this family. Sue and Ben are living their X-treme dreams together and have been able to bless others because of that abundance. God wants you to prosper in **every area of your life.**

I'd also like to tell you about a grandmother named Linda. She had a burning desire to be used in the area of drama. Her heart ached to be an actress. Yet she believed it was too late for her to step out into an X-treme dream. How could someone her age dream at all? After all, isn't dreaming just for young people? NO WAY!

Linda sat down with me one day to learn how to use the grid. In less than two years, she was not only acting, but touring and teaching

Vision Grid

	Immediate (Primary) Now	Near Term (Secondary) 1-6 Months	X-treme Dream Long Term (Luxury) 1-5 Years	Bible Verses
Vision *(blue-print for my life: what keeps me up at at night)*				*Habakkuk 2:2-4* *Hebrews 11:1-3* *Psalms 139:13-16*
Burdens of the Heart *(pet projects)*				*Proverbs 20:18* *Proverbs 27:17* *Proverbs 11:14* *Jeremiah 29: 11-13*
Responsibilities *(natural world, e.g., work, health)*				*I Corinthians 2: 9-10* *Proverbs 18:16* *Proberbs 22:29*

Tips for success

1. Do something for your vision each day.
2. Be ruthless with your time, and not with people.
3. Check your grid every 3 to 6 months.
4. Get an accountability team.

God loves me more than the vision to which He has called me.

others in a small college how to act! Our God does not see age or time in the same way you and I do. All you need to do is be willing to take the leap of faith when He says jump! Are **you** ready?

One of John Wayne's famous films is called "True Grit." The character depicted by John Wayne was a drunken, one-eyed US marshal who was looking for a killer. Just like Wayne's character in the film, people who show brave perseverance or stubborn courage are thought to have true grit. **You** have true grit because you are now embarking on your own vision quest. Being a person of true grit means that you must discover your true grid. No, that's not a typo. The next thing you need to visualize is your personal Vision Grid.

Now that you've had time to reconnect with the original blueprint God designed for you, you can place the bits and pieces of information you've rediscovered into the Vision Grid on the previous page. The grid allows you to see your vision laid out in bite-sized chunks.

So pull out a pencil and let's take a look at the vertical information of the grid first. As you look at the first box on the far left of the grid, you see the word **Vision**. This first row of boxes is going to hold the pieces of your overall vision. Remember that your vision is the original, God-ordained, custom-designed blueprint for your life. Parts of your vision are to be written in each of the three boxes in the first row.

I suggest that you place one to three doable actions in each of the three boxes in that row. Now go back to your brainstorming sheets and your treasure map and begin to put some order to the things/ideas previously written. Go from the most doable action to what you think might be the most farfetched action or idea. Place the wildest thing in the last box on the far right, because that is the **X-treme Dream** column.

Now go back to each box and put dates for completion by each action. The more specific you are, the more specific God will be with you.

Take a look at the column marked **Immediate** or **Primary**. This is for the actions in each category that you believe to be the most immediate and accessible to you in your vision. You can begin these right away.

Before you do that, however, I'd like for you to consider God's picture of time, because it is quite different from ours. To Him, one day is a thousand years, and a thousand years is a day (2 Peter 3:8). He must have the freedom in your life to do as He wills with the things you place on your grid. You can have a plan, but it is the Lord who will establish it (Proverbs 16:9). God can cause things to happen SUDDENLY when you place your dreams in His hands, although this doesn't always mean quickly. God often causes things to happen when you least expect them. That's called a suddenly. Let me explain.

When I filled in my first grid, I thought my desire would take five years to become a reality, so that's the date I placed by all the goals God had put on my heart. But God completed everything on my first grid in 10 months! These were not small desires either, no siree! One of them was the desire for a movie-critic TV show called "Reel Sisters" that would cost thousands of dollars to produce. I had not one dime in the bank to do it, but I didn't need to have the money right then. God had the money, and He caused a series of "suddenlies" to happen that made the TV show a reality.

Isn't our God the One who owns every animal in the forest and the cattle on a thousand hills (Psalm 50:10)? You bet He is! In 2000, my sister Shaunya (now a seasoned screenwriter and playwright) and I received a national award for that show.

But then again, I thought the settlement for a car accident I was in would be settled quickly because it was a DUI on the part of the other driver and everything seemed to be in place to settle. Well, the accident happened over five years ago and I am still waiting for God's hand to move on that situation. Is God on vacation? Absolutely not! He is working out that whole circumstance in His way and on His heavenly time clock. I can't be worried and neither can you as you wait. **Trust is key.** Okay, now let's go back to your grid work.

The **Near Term**, or **Secondary** column, is for the activities you see yourself doing once the items in the Immediate column begin to happen. These desires are farther out in the time line.

The last column is marked **X-treme Dream** or **Long Term** for all those things in each category you'd want to achieve *if you knew there was* *no way for you to fail.* This column is where God's greatness shines through you in an extraordinary way. It is here that your lifelong dreams and visions become a reality. This is the time or season in your life where God shows Himself strongly to you. As you begin to jot down your actions for this column, ask yourself, "What would I be or do if I knew I'd never fail?" The possibilities are endless because we serve a big God. Each one of us is a success story waiting to happen!

During the process of filling in your Vision Grid, you may feel overwhelmed. That's okay. Take a deep breath and ask the Lord to speak to you about how to fill in the boxes for each category and part of the time line, keeping in mind that you can be flexible and change things as needed later. (Remember you've already spent time alone with Him thinking out of the box for every area of your life.) Keep your hand in His hand and remind yourself that you are partnered with Him in this process. All of heaven is cheering you on as you step out and take a courageous leap of faith with Him to carry out your vision and begin living the X-treme dream.

As you give yourself permission to expose these parts of your vision, before God and the entire universe, you are making a declaration about your true self and your inheritance. God designed us with a purpose and a plan for good, not evil, before we were even born (Jeremiah 29:11, Psalm 139:13-16). How amazing is that? Your true grid defines how and why you are fearfully and wonderfully made (Psalm 139:14). The vision God designed for you to fulfill cannot be fulfilled by anyone but you because you are so unique.

A very talented writer recently told me that she didn't think it was right for her to write a devotional book because so many others had already written devotional books. She didn't see how her devotional book would make any difference. I felt horrible for her, because what she failed to realize was that God has writers and artists of all sorts. Each one has a distinct vision, voice and role to play in His divine production. I mean, what if Luciano Pavarotti decided not to sing anymore because he thought Andrea Bocelli was better? What a tragic loss that would be!

When you are filling in the boxes of your Vision Grid, remember not to compare yourself with anyone. Put away small thinking; and dream BIG and think NEW! God has so much waiting for us on the other side of our obedience to His still, small voice.

He has promised us the X-treme dream. No one has seen, thought or heard what God has already prepared for us (1 Corinthians 2:9-10).

PSALM 84:11

For the Lord God is a sun and shield; the Lord bestows favor and honor; no good thing does He withhold from those whose walk is blameless.

Staying on our vertical train of thought, let's look at the box below Vision. It's labeled **Burdens of the Heart** or **Pet Projects**. In Chapter One we discussed this category as one of the two groups of things that can distract us from accomplishing our X-treme dream and vision.

Burdens of the heart are your pet projects; they can be hobbies or leftover pieces of the overall vision. Only you can decide what God is telling to your heart about the pieces of your vision and what you will put into each box of the grid.

Take a look at your notes from your quiet time. See anything that might be placed in the three boxes of the Burdens row? You're using a pencil, so it's fine to jot something down and then rearrange the items as you go along. You want to follow the same thought process you used when you were filling in the Vision row.

Start with the simplest actions first and move all the way across to the third box with the actions you feel are the most difficult to accomplish. Remember to go back and put specific deadlines (day, month and year) for yourself with each action. The third box should always reflect your highest aspirations. Hold nothing back here. God loves to make possible what seems impossible to us.

It's important to note that what you write in the boxes can be tangible or intangible. Some people have taken the seminar with me and discovered that their prosperity needed to come from intangible relationships being healed within a family or group of friends. Others have very distinct financial goals they've decided to work on with God. Get quiet enough with God to let Him speak to you, and then be bold enough to write it down.

Now you're ready to tackle the row for all of your **Responsibilities**. Going back to our definitions in Chapter One, we see that these are the day-to-day activities we must do in the natural, tangible world.

Take a look at all the areas you are responsible for taking care of in your family or on your job. Make a list of all these responsibilities and number them like you did in the other rows. Save the wildest and seemingly most difficult activities for last and place them in the last column for your X-treme dream space.

Remember that this is the place to put all those tangible items from your weekly, monthly or annual to-do list. This is a major area to pay close attention to because this is where most of us live. This is the area in most people's lives that takes so much of their time that there is usually no energy left for them to walk out God's dream or vision for them.

It is no accident that **Vision** is placed in the first row and **Responsibilities** are placed in the last row. The Lord wants us to seek His vision for our lives *first* and foremost. Why? An English teacher of mine in high school once said, "The world is too much with us!" This is so true. We live with such cares of the tangible. God wants us to think instead on His plans and the future He has designed for us.

Does God care about this tangible world we live in? Absolutely! He tells us this in Matthew 6:26-27:

Look at the birds of the air; they do not sow or reap or store away in barns, and yet your heavenly Father feeds them. Are you not much more valuable than they? Who of you by worrying can add a single hour to his life?

God has everything under control and our best interests at the center of His heart. Not just some things. *Everything*. And He wants us to cast all our cares, big and small, on Him because He cares about everything that concerns us.

Matthew 10:30-31

And even the very hairs of your head are all numbered. So don't be afraid; you are worth more than many sparrows.

If we'll just ask Him, He'll provide the solution to every problem and the provision for every need. Can you consider His perspective on your life and trust Him in a fresh new way? He desires to walk with you into a place too large and superb to contain all He has for you (Psalm 18:19, 36). Give the responsibilities and the worries of your soul to the Lord. He has peace for the chaos we sometimes find ourselves in.

Now I'd like to lead you through some sets of specific actions you can take throughout your life on a daily basis to ensure the fulfillment of your X-treme dream.

CHAPTER 4

YOU CAN HAVE X-TREME VISION EVERY DAY

Dream as though you were to live forever.
Live as though you were to die tomorrow.
— ANONYMOUS

When we are obedient to what God has called us to do, we can rest, because we know the results are not our responsibility – they're God's. Each day we present our tasks to God and rely upon Him to give us the strength we need to complete them.
— STACEY S. PADRICK

To be excellent, you have to be consistent.
— TOM PETERS

Set high goals for the best-ALWAYS.
— ANONYMOUS

Take the first step in faith.
You don't have to see the whole staircase, just take the first step.
— DR. MARTIN LUTHER KING, JR.

Have you ever wondered what would happen if **everyone** in the world lived from their visions every day? Pause for a moment and think on that. What great things could you accomplish if you had your vision before you every day of your life? Is it possible to live like that? *Absolutely*!

God gives us guidance on how to do it, but first we have to understand what His word says to us regarding vision. Let's take another look at:

HABAKKUK 2:2-3

And the Lord answered me and said, Write the vision and engrave it so plainly upon tablets that everyone who passes may [be able to] read [it easily and quickly] as he hastens by. For the vision is yet for an appointed time and it hastens to the end [fulfillment]; it will not deceive or disappoint. Though it tarry, wait [earnestly] for it, because it will surely come; it will not be behindhand on its appointed day.

Now go to your Vision Grid and look at what you've filled in for each part of your vision. Take time to realize the goals you've set and the dates by which you want to complete them. Can you see yourself completing these goals?

As you reflect on these goals, you might be thinking lots of different things about yourself at this time in your life. Let's take a moment to undo anything that could hinder you.

Jot down 10 positive and true things about yourself and vow, right now, to always believe them.

1. ______________________________

2. ______________________________

3. ______________________________

4.____
5.____
6.____
7.____
8.____
9.____
10.____

Now take a moment to write down all of the myths you have believed about yourself and ask the Lord to take them away from your thoughts.

1.____
2.____
3.____
4.____

This exercise is vital because we must get a picture of how the Lord sees us before the X-treme dream can become a reality. Our thought life is crucial for the results we want to live out and the goals we want to accomplish before the Lord. That's why the Apostle Paul gave us this exhortation in:

PHILIPPIANS 4:8

Finally, brothers, whatever is true, whatever is noble, whatever is right, whatever is pure, whatever is lovely, whatever is admirable-if anything is excellent or praiseworthy-think about such things.

At a critical point in my life, I had the opportunity to try this verse out. It happened when I was a junior in college. I was an A student through all my years of school and had a great love for anything dealing with communication, language or English. So I signed up for a senior-level English course for a good challenge.

The course was taught by a Ph.D. from Drake University, and I don't think any of us in that lecture hall had any idea what a difficult ride we were in for that semester. We started with an enrollment of about 60 students but, by the end of the semester, there were only about 15 of us left. It was one of the most grueling courses I'd ever had.

One day, after I turned in a paper the professor didn't like, she asked to see me out in the hall for a moment. There she told me that she had heard of my dream of wanting to become a journalist and author someday. She said, "Charlynne, I hate to tell you this, but I honestly don't believe you have what it takes to be a journalist or writer."

I remember being first hurt and then shocked that a professor at my beloved school would say something so daunting to an exemplary student like me. When I got back to my dormitory, I made a conscious decision to think on what the Lord God said about me. And from that day on, I vowed to never let anyone define who I was or who they thought I could become.

One year after graduating with honors, I began working at a national magazine as the associate editor. Six years after that, I served as the lead press officer for a White House assignment. If I had allowed one woman's superficial opinion of my abilities to take root in my life, I would never have had the strength or courage to live out the X-treme dream God had already designed for me. And you can bet that I certainly wouldn't be writing this book right now! *No one is qualified to define you but God Himself!*

God does not play favorites and we must follow His lead. Getting His perspective on who you really are trains your thoughts to line up with His thoughts. This must become a daily habit.

Every time I've been able to articulate a dream to those I trust, that dream has come true. Telling someone close to and very trusted by you what your vision is solidifies your own inner declaration and helps make you work toward making what you've spoken become a reality. There is such power in what we say! Scripture tells us in James 3:10 that there is blessing and cursing in our tongues. So let's choose to bless with every word that comes out of our mouths. Our words have an impact on our dreams and what God has planned for us.

Over the years, I have gained the habit of dedicating a portion of every day to working on the overall vision or X-treme dream for my life. You might think this an impossible feat, but it isn't. It doesn't matter how much time you have to dedicate to this each day. What matters is your **consistency** in doing it. You must make the time you set aside for your X-treme dream sacred. Let no person or thing hinder you in your sacred time. God will honor you when you do it.

This simple truth brings to mind the quandary I found myself in when I decided I wanted to lead a drama team on a tour of England for an entire summer. I was just about to graduate from college and I needed $3,500 for my portion of the trip. Since I had no money, I got quiet and asked God what to do about the situation. I felt He wanted me to make the trip and so I desperately needed to hear His voice speak to me. As I prayed, I felt He was leading me to earn my way to England, through the sale of homemade cookies. Enter problem number two. The recipe I wanted to borrow from my stepmother could not be found! So I went back to the Lord and, as I sat quietly, I felt Him say that I could create my own recipe.

Well, here I was in my final semester of school. I had so much on my plate that this seemed like an impossible task. Before I could even think of creating a new recipe, I had to defend my senior TV project in order to walk with honors, deliver my daily drive-time newscast at a local Tulsa radio station, and continue as the resident advisor for 32 young women! How in the world was I going to find the time to not only create a new recipe but bake the cookies as well?

Consistency was the key. I went to class every day, did my advisor duties and delivered my newscast. By the time I got back to the dorm, it would be dark and very late. I then did my class work and checked in on my girls. Then, about 1 AM every night, I experimented with a cookie recipe to knock people's socks off. I was praying that God would anoint me as a baker.

At the end of two weeks of **consistently** baking at one in the morning, I created a recipe I thought would sell. Well, good word spreads fast, and the cookies were a huge hit with the students. The comforting aroma of my cookies brought people to my dorm room with cash in hand.

Soon there was a newspaper article about my baked goods and the reporter printed my phone number. Hundreds of orders began to come in. The early-morning baking ritual had to continue because the demand was so great! My gourmet oatmeal-raisin and oatmeal-chocolate chip cookies had just the right amount of brown sugar and cinnamon, and a secret mix of flour to make them rise very high yet stay soft and chewy.

Ten weeks had passed since I first felt like I was supposed to bake my way to England and I had raised over $10,000. That was more than enough for me and another person on my drama team to do missions for an entire summer — with spending money, too.

When I got back from England, I decided to create a catering company called Charlie's Chewies. It was a perfect way to combine my love of creating delicious food, meeting people and coordinating special events. I learned very quickly that a sacred time, where I consistently worked on a dream, could have dramatic effects on my life and the lives of others.

Please set aside some time for yourself each day to work on your vision and dreams. I promise you won't regret it. Give yourself the permission to dream often and dream *big*! And be sure to display something from your treasure map on your refrigerator door or most-used mirror. In this way, you can think on your dream and keep it before you every day.

Another way to live your X-treme dream every day is to celebrate when large or small goals from your dream become a reality. This is an absolute must! It's so easy to work hard to reach an achievement and then keep pushing on to the next milestone. Don't. Relax and enjoy your victories and successes.

Remembering our past victories is an age-old biblical truth that ensures more success. You want to be sure to make memories you can pull out and draw upon during the tough times. One of the best ways to build strength is to be able to encourage ourselves when the going gets tough. That's how David conquered Goliath. He recounted his past victories whenever he faced challenges and continued to succeed throughout his life. God moves on impossible situations when He hears us rehearsing our victories. He is only too happy to show up on the scene and make sure everything turns out right.

Rehearsing past victories is just as important as celebrating recent achievements. When my cousin Laurel received her first Emmy Award as a TV producer, my sister and I screamed with joy when we got the news. We were so thrilled for her! Earlier in the year, she had written down that she wanted to win an Emmy Award. And in X-treme dream style, we decided to treat her to dinner at the famous Palm Restaurant. But wait! We didn't just take her. We took her Emmy, too — one that was divinely bestowed upon her.

Every Palm Restaurant has a heart for celebrities in the entertainment industry. And that night was no different. We put the Emmy on the table and every person who walked by congratulated her. It was a night she'll never forget. Now she's got a memory of celebration she can tuck away and pull out at will. She was queen for the night and thoroughly enjoyed her time in the spotlight. I can't emphasize enough how important taking the time to celebrate a victory is to the success of a vision.

Do you have stray thoughts or impressions in your waking and/or sleeping moments? If so, keep a pad of paper in your pocket and by your bed to capture those thoughts. If you get a vivid dream that stays on your mind, after you wake up, write it down. Or maybe you have recurring dreams about yourself in specific places or doing specific activities. Jot these down, too. God might be trying to get your attention about something having to do with your vision or what's on your treasure map.

It's time for the "suddenlies" of life to happen to you. Just by agreeing to begin this process, by partnering with the Lord and standing on His word, you are allowing Him to unleash all the resources of heaven on your behalf.

We have no idea what all God can do in just one day's time, so let's make sure we have positioned ourselves to hear His voice and be all that

He says we already are. The Lord is giving us a God's-eye view of what He put within us. It's as if each of us is a supernatural time capsule waiting to be opened. **Why not you? Why not now?**

The topic of time is the next stop on our X-treme journey. On we go!

Chapter 5

The X Factor: Being Ruthless with your Time

We want God's timing for the maximum effect!
— Shaunya Boddie

Time is the most valuable thing that a man can spend.
— Theophrastus

While we wait for tomorrow, we must act for today.
— Meni Sivasubramanian

My times are in Your hands; deliver me from the hands of my foes and those who pursue me and persecute me.
— King David, Psalm 31:15

Several years ago, while I was on vacation in England, God spoke to me through the wisdom of two friends. I was just getting ready to return to the States when my friend, Helen, and her husband, Simon, took me out to dinner. She said that she had been praying for me and had a word from the Lord for me.

There was nothing unusual about that, because Helen and Simon are two of my oldest friends in England. They both agreed to pray for me and the vision for my life on a constant basis. So I listened to what Helen felt the Lord wanted her to say to me.

Helen began by telling me that she believed 70% of my contacts and acquaintances were about to disappear. She went on to say that the loss of these contacts would not be because of arguments or conflicts, but that those relationships would just end once I got back to the States. She felt God didn't want me to chase after the relationships I'd lose, but instead wanted me to accept that it would happen.

Well, talk about having the wind knocked out of you! I was very concerned when I heard these words. Yet I knew Helen had my best interests at heart and I knew that was doubly so of God. I decided to take those words to the Lord in prayer as soon as possible. Our lovely Indian meal ended and we went to an evening church service nearby where I was greeted by another friend, Amanda. She and her husband, Paul, have also prayed for me on various occasions and she, too, felt that she needed to share something God had said.

Can you guess what Amanda said? She said that the Lord advised her to tell me about the 30/70 Rule! (Mind you, Amanda and Paul had not spoken to Helen and Simon. The two couples didn't even know one another.) Interestingly enough, Amanda had the same interpretation of 30 and 70 ratio that Helen had given me three hours earlier! This was too much to be a coincidence, and it showed me how very jealous God is of my time! I realized He craves time with me and you because what

He wants most from us is a **relationship**.

God was telling me to cut back on my social life so He and I could spend more quality time with each other. He used two dear friends to tell me. WOW! Good stewardship of time is just as important to the Lord as good stewardship of money. What we do with our time can make or break the success of our X-treme dream. **We must be ruthless with time, not people.**

There is a way to multiply our time without hurting those around us, but first we must get an accurate snapshot of what we're doing with our time. This leads me to a challenge for you. Please stop right now and make a note to yourself to keep a three-day diary of how you're spending your time. This sample period will tell you where your time is going and with whom you are spending it. The key here is honesty. Be honest with yourself and jot down, from morning to night, what you are doing with your time. Show me where and how you spend your time and I'll show you why your dreams have not yet come true.

The wonderful thing about this exercise is that once you see where your time is going, *you can correct it*. Your choices are always there. Choose to make the very most of your time and God will honor you in the process.

Once you have completed your three-day diary, ask yourself if there are any relationships you need to let go of or change. If there are people draining your time and hindering the flow of your vision and God's purposes for your life, *let them go* with God's blessing.

When I returned from my trip to England, I wondered how this revelation would pan out. Part of me didn't want to lose 70 percent the names in my big book. But I knew God had spoken and I knew I wanted Him more than anything else, so I released those names and contacts, never looking back. I moved forward with the 30% God said I could have and my life has been blessed as a result. Releasing the time-drainers made room for the relationships God *did* want me to have. Remember, **the Lord always has your best interests at heart**. That's what the Lord asked of me. What is He asking of you?

3-Day Time Diary

	Day One	**Two**	**Three**
6:00 AM			
7:00			
8:00			
9:00			
10:00			
11:00			
Noon			
1:00 PM			
2:00			
3:00			
4:00			
5:00			
6:00			
7:00			
8:00			
9:00			
10:00			
11:00			
Midnight			

Relationships/Activities

Who/What to Add?	**Who/What to Delete?**

Just as God may be asking you to take stock of what doesn't need to be in your life, He may also point out some things or people He does want in your life. Be open to His still, small voice telling you about additions as you make time by deleting what may be unhealthy for you.

The key is to constantly ask yourself if how you're spending your time gets you closer to fulfilling your X-treme dream. Ask this question for all your activities and all your relationships. You may need to make some changes. If some "spring cleaning" needs to take place in your life, do it with joy. Realize that every change is an investment in your X-treme dream and a more intimate relationship with your Lord and Savior.

In being ruthless with your time, be sure to take inventory on your vision, the burdens of your heart and your real-world responsibilities. God wants you to prosper in all three areas (3 John verse 2). Balancing your time allows you to have more time with the Lord and move closer to the fruition of your dreams. And God will multiply time back to you in ways you never thought possible.

One company, Pampered Chef, has made meal-preparation time much shorter by offering kitchen tools that cut the time you spend cooking. This is just one example of a "witty invention" (Proverbs 8:12 in the King James Bible) that Pampered Chef founder Doris Christopher developed for her vision. When we get serious with the Lord and how we use our time, He gets serious with us and reveals things that were previously unknown.

Know that whatever needs to be done regarding how you spend your time, God will make a way for the necessary changes. He is the Master of time and sees such things with spiritual eyes. You can too, by just calling on His name to help you sort out where you are in this area of your life. You can manage your time instead of it managing you.

How much time are you spending with the Lord? Do you have special time set aside just for Him to communicate with you and you with Him? If time with Him is absent from your schedule, get quiet before the Lord and ask Him when and how you are to spend time with Him. **Make that time sacred**. Allow nothing and no one to encroach on your special time with God. As I said before, *consistency is key* here. Go ahead and write down when, where and how you plan to spend time with the Lord. This is your **God Spot**.

God Spot Facts

When: ______________________________

Where: ______________________________

How: ______________________________

JAMES 4:8

Come near to God and He will come near to you…

The pursuit of your visions and dreams must never replace your relationship with the Lord. Partnering with Him during the journey makes for a true joy ride. Make sure you always take Him with you in whatever you do and wherever you go. Seek His presence more than His presents and He'll give you the pleasure of His company and more!

My sincere prayer in writing this book is that you will gain intimacy with the Lord as you walk down the road of life. And that in doing so, your desires will mirror His desires for you. How you spend your time and with whom you spend it are at the core of God's plan for your X-treme dream. It is never too late to get His perspective on this topic. In the next chapter, we'll look at how to focus while you're on the journey.

CHAPTER 6

CHECKING IN WITH HIS X-CELLENCY THE MOST HIGH GOD, CREATOR OF YOUR DREAM

In order to know what to say, you have to get in touch with those deep-inside-of-you thoughts, feelings, needs and yearnings.
— DR. NEIL WARREN

God doesn't want our success; He wants us.
He doesn't demand our achievements; He demands our obedience.
— CHUCK COLSON

Success is not final. Failure is not fatal.
It is the courage to continue that counts.
— SIR WINSTON CHURCHILL

Most people achieved their greatest successes one step beyond what looked like their greatest failure.
— BRIAN TRACY

I became a cartoonist largely because I failed in my goal of becoming a successful executive.
— SCOTT ADAMS OF "DILBERT" FAME

Along the road of the X-treme dream journey, it can be easy to get so caught up in all you'll see and do that you might forget to check in with the Chief Architect of your blueprint. God wants to communicate with you throughout the journey; not just at the beginning and end of your dream.

While Jesus walked on the earth, I believe His X-treme dream was to carry out the will of His Father and reunite mankind with God, tearing down the barriers once and for all. He always checked in with "headquarters" and made time to talk with His Father. We need to follow His lead and do the same.

At this stage of your X-treme dream journey, you need to evaluate where you are at least every three to six months, to see if you are on track with the vision God has created for you. Take a good look at all the parts of your vision and ask yourself if you need to make adjustments in any area.

This is also the time to acknowledge whether or not you have celebrated the completion of your goals along the way. It's important to celebrate as you reach your goals, because victories are the fuel you can use to encourage yourself when storms come. I keep a journal just to record all my victories. And when the rain comes, and you know it will, you can pull out your list of victories and relive them. That builds you up on the inside and reminds you that the Lord is on the job, working with you throughout the journey. God loves to hear His children revisit what He's done in our lives.

Take a moment to jot down some of your victories. Go back as far as you can remember and move forward to this place and time in your life. Every victory, small or large, deserves to be celebrated. List them here.

Victories

____

____

Now ask yourself if you took time out to celebrate those victories. If so, jot down how you celebrated your victories. If not, write down how you'd like to celebrate your next victory. Plan out who will be there, where you'll do it and when it will be. Be specific!

Celebrations

Celebrations vary from culture to culture. In the Navajo Indian culture, parties are thrown for babies when they laugh for the first time. Isn't that special? Experiencing joy is such an important part of living. Scripture says that the joy of the Lord is our strength (Nehemiah 8:10). As we celebrate the handiwork of God in our lives and along the journey to fulfillment of our dreams and visions, He brings us more joy and cause to celebrate. We are talking about living with a cup that overflows with the fullness only God can give.

Another great thing about this stage of the X-treme dream journey is the fact that you may, after taking inventory of your vision, see that the Lord has already begun to work in all nine squares of your Vision

Grid. You may be thinking, "Are you crazy, Charlynne?"

No, I don't think so. Although it might be hard to fathom that every area of your grid may be coming into fruition, I tell you *it can* and *it will* if you will take God at His word. He never lies and He is always faithful.

I previously told you about a couple with a large family who had been laid off from their jobs. The goals of the Browns' first Vision Grid occurred in about two years. Once that happened, they began to *dream again with God*. Both spouses took stock of where they were and celebrated their victories. Then they began setting goals for the next leg of their X-treme dream. When those goals became reality, they kept on going. They are living the dream while keeping the process in tact. Guess what? *If they can do it, you can, too!*

I am constantly updating and adjusting my own Vision Grid. I'm on my fourth grid and am moving toward the middle of the grid in all three areas. All the primary column goals have been met. The key word is *forward*. As long as you keep moving forward, *one step at a time, nothing can stop you.*

The possibilities are endless. Yes, bottomless. You belong to the Mastermind behind the creation of the entire universe! Listen to:

PSALM 46:10

Be still, and know that I am God. I will be exalted among the nations, I will be exalted in the earth.

Remember that God's creativity is limitless. As soon as each bite-sized goal becomes a reality, *keep on dreaming*. Write your extended vision on another grid. Realize that, with the God you serve, **all** possibilities for living the X-treme dream are infinite. *Any and every thing is possible!*

If you have thoughts pertaining to your extended vision percolating in your mind, write them here. It doesn't need to be a full or complete thought yet; it can simply be an idea, word, phrase or picture. Just having the courage to write it breathes life into the next part of your dream. These notations will be the seeds for your next Vision Grid. Go for it!

X-tended Vision Ideas

The previous chapters helped you tap into your relationship with God. Chapter Seven will show you how to develop better earthly relationships, which are essential to living your X-treme dream.

Chapter 7

Adding to the X-treme Equation: Your Accountability Team

Learn to listen. Opportunity could be knocking at your door very softly.
— Frank Tyger

There is no such thing as a self-made man. We are made up of thousands of others. Everyone who has ever done a kind deed for us, or spoken one word of encouragement to us, has entered into the makeup of our character and of our thoughts, as well as our success.
— George Matthew Adams

Accountability makes us check the motives behind our activities.
— Anonymous

One learns people through the heart; not the eyes or the intellect.
— Mark Twain

Quality relationships take time. Relational depth is often a casualty in a hurry-sick world that glorifies exhaustion as a badge of accomplishment and accepts shallow relationships as a necessary price of achieving our individual ambitions.
— Tim Muelhoff

Life is a theater… Invite your audience carefully.
— Anonymous

Academy Awards are given every March for the most outstanding achievements in film. As the winners receive their Oscars, they usually have a long acceptance speech prepared for that special moment. Those of us watching at home hear a litany of names, known and unknown, that each winner wants to publicly recognize. Hardly anyone accepts the award on his or her own merit. Credit is always given to the *team* of individuals who helped make their moment in the spotlight possible.

If you were nominated for an award and won, who would you publicly thank? Let me put it another way. Who are your cheerleaders? Write your list of people here:

Your Personal Cheerleaders

____

____

____

____

____

____

____

I want to talk to you about the importance of *accountability* in your life. You need a team of people you can be accountable to as you walk out your X-treme dream. *They are your personal A-Team.*

Why? Meditate on these verses of wisdom:

PROVERBS 15:22
Plans fail for lack of counsel but, with many advisers, they succeed.

PROVERBS 20:18
Make plans by seeking advice; if you wage war, obtain guidance.

PROVERBS 24:5-6
A wise man has great power, and a man of knowledge increases strength; for waging war you need guidance, and for victory many advisors.

This whole book is showing you how to "wage war" against the enemy by strategizing with all God's tools and resources, so that you will be able to grow into all you were originally designed to be. You are not meant to do this alone. The first person on you're A-Team is God, of course. Now let's look at how to go about developing the rest of your team.

You have already compiled a list of people who support you. That's terrific! Some or all of them may be great candidates for your personal team. Before we ponder those names, let's look at the duties of A-Team members.

A-Team Duties

1. Prayer for the X-treme dreamer (you)
2. A check-in from time to time to see how you are doing on your journey
3. Mentoring as needed
4. Advice as needed
5. Honesty at all times and possible correction
6. Confidentiality at all times
7. Willingness to listen and celebrate your successes and milestones

You will have duties to each team member as well. This can't be a one-way street. You must reciprocate in your relationship with your teammates. Here's your list:

Dreamer Duties

1. Pray for each A-Team member
2. Provide timely updates on your journey toward the dream
3. *Listen* to your team's wisdom
4. Be honest with the team at all times
5. Keep their confidences
6. Celebrate your team members' successes
7. Walk in an attitude of gratitude for the investment *each* teammate has made in your life

Prayer is one of the most important things you can do for each other. Making a commitment to actively pray for one another is one of the surest ways to quench the fiery darts of the enemy. Pray without ceasing (1 Thessalonians 5:17).

God says we are waging war when we make plans or strategize. You may be doing just that when you launch your X-treme dream journey, because the last thing the enemy of your soul wants is for you to partner with God or anyone else to begin living your X-treme dream. Then you are a serious threat to all of his diabolical schemes.

The previous lists tell you and anyone who is interested in being a part of your team what is expected of them. Next, you must get very quiet before the Lord and seek His advice on who you should approach about being on your team. Ask a small group of godly people you feel you can trust with your heart's secret petitions if they'd like to be on your A-Team. This is serious business folks. You can't ask just anyone. These people should be right with both God and man, and foster healthy relationships.

When the Lord gives you peace about your list of candidates, invite them in person if at all possible. If they live out of state, call or mail a letter to them explaining your request. Use email only as a last resort.

There is no magic number of people for your team. It should be more than one and probably less than eight or nine. Remember, you want to be accountable to your team and also be able to have meaningful relationships with each member.

Half of my team is in the States and half is overseas. Counting all the spouses, there are nine people on my A-Team. Modern technology, travel, and our commitment to each other makes it work. What a blessing they all are to me! All of the members of my A-team have spoken wisdom and truth over my life at the most amazing times.

Some of you may have an inclination to ask someone you don't know well to share in this responsibility. Perhaps the person(s) you are thinking of has certain skills or a body of knowledge you'd like to glean from. That is up to you and the Lord to decide. You can check it out with other A-Team members who you have known longer as well. It is possible to have a person on your team for a season or a very specific need. Ask God to tell you who you should consider each step of the way. He will answer you. Don't be shy about asking these people either. Be obedient to **whatever** God says.

Before I go further, I must stress the importance of **prayer** when choosing your A-Team members. Let God open the doors and you won't be sorry. Wait on Him to tell you who to ask. You must have wisdom in choosing who to share your heart with. Not everyone should hear the secrets of your X-treme dream; they must be godly people! It is a precious set of blueprints and it must be treated as such.

My friend Aaron began his X-treme dream journey two years ago. He is a brilliant aerospace engineer with a doctorate from MIT and a Master of Divinity on top of that. This man excels at almost anything he tries. Despite his successes, he wanted more of God in his life than anything else.

One of the areas that intrigued this man of many talents was the A-Team process. Aaron knew that, because of his genius intelligence level, he could very easily choose not to be accountable to anyone. He knew that one of his weak spots was his dependence on himself and his own strength.

So Aaron decided to seek God's face about becoming more **inter-dependent** on Him. He asked God who he should be accountable to in his everyday life as he moved toward the fulfillment of his vision.

Aaron came up with a list of men and women who agreed to come together a few times a year and pray individually over Aaron's life and X-treme dream. As the facilitator of these team gatherings, I can tell you that Aaron is a changed person. He is so much more conscious of areas where he can improve, and now he is not alone in doing it! He has a loving team of supporters who are cheering him on from the sidelines. Aaron and his teammates recognize that God is their Head Coach. I act as the assistant coach and Aaron's supporters are the team players.

Now, are you ready to jot down the names of some potential A-Team members for your X-treme dream game plan? (You can have singles or couples.)

Potential A-Team Members

1. ______________________________
2. ______________________________
3. ______________________________
4. ______________________________
5. ______________________________
6. ______________________________

Once you've contacted each person or couple, wait to hear his or her response. Place a star or circle on every name that says yes. Then send each of your A-Team members a copy of your Vision Grid. Ask them all to pray over it and stand in agreement with you that it will become a reality in God's way and timing. Be sure to ask each team member how you can pray for them. Remember, this is a two-way street. You are building solid, meaningful relationships within the body of Christ.

Begin to communicate with your A-Team consistently. Provide quarterly updates in person, by phone or through email. You can even do what Aaron does and schedule dinner meetings in your home. You can be as creative as you want. Get the pulse of your particular team and go from there.

Be sure to include your A-Team in all of your celebrations, too.

That way you are all experiencing your successes together. You can praise God for what He is doing together!

Honor the advice and time your team members give you. You have already read what God says about the wisdom of counselors. Their advice is a choice gift to you and the fulfillment of your X-treme dream. These men and women are essentially the "cabinet" or "board" for YOU, Inc. Remember to be gracious and thankful to these people you will partner with. They are going to invest the best part of themselves into you *and* your dream. God has given them to you for your success and safety.

The more you seek quality, respect, growth, peace of mind, love and truth around you, the easier it will become for you to decide who gets to sit in the front row and who should be moved to the balcony of your life. Remember that the people we hang with will have an impact on both our lives and our income.

As you travel down the road of your X-treme dream adventure, you need to be aware of what to expect so you can be proactive in all you do and become. Chapter Eight gives you ten road signs to watch for.

Chapter 8

Releasing the X-treme Dream: What You Can Expect

When you're consistent, you're vulnerable to attack.
Yes, it's a paradox. Now deal with it!
— Tom Peters

The jewels of a Christian are his afflictions . . . Griefs exalt us and troubles lift us up. [If we suffer, we shall also reign with Him.]
— C.H. Spurgeon

During perilous times, innovation is not just a good idea;
it is a necessity for survival.
— Terry Brock

The spirit, the will to win, and the will to excel are the things that endure.
These qualities are so much more important than the events that occur.
— Vince Lombardi

God wants to put His "super" on your "natural!"
— Pastor Rufus Thibodeaux

Now that you are well on your way to living out your X-treme dream, you must be prepared for what lies ahead. There are ten road signs you can expect to see along the journey.

I am reminded of what a popular stand-up comedian/movie star once said about his new title of "#1 comedian in America." He said, "It was awful and wonderful all at once. Getting to the top of any field is a terrific feat, *but* staying on top is altogether different. Why? Because once you get to the coveted position, there is always someone there who wants to knock you off!"

Road Sign #1: Spiritual Attacks

Your enemy, Satan, prowls around like a roaring lion, seeking anyone he may devour (1 Peter 5:8). You are especially tempting to him when you realize what your vision and destiny are. You, my friend, are now a threat to the enemy's camp. He would love to knock you off your course and cause you to drop your X-treme dream and any thoughts for the completion of it.

The Lord does not want us to be surprised by this in any way. You must expect a fight from the enemy and be prepared to war with him over the fulfillment of your X-treme dream. You and I are hated by this enemy of our souls, and God wants us to be prepared for oppression. Our trials help us to develop as mature believers and dreamers. Think on this:

JAMES 1:2-4

Consider it pure joy, my brothers, whenever you face trials of many kinds, because you know that the testing of your faith develops perseverance. Perseverance must finish its work so that you may be mature and complete, not lacking anything.

Road Sign #2: Naysayers or Dream Stealers

Have you encountered anyone on your X-treme dream journey who verbally shot down your dream? That is a naysayer, a potential dream stealer. You may have even come across several, depending on how many people have heard your vision or dream. This is why it's so important to ask the Lord with whom and when you can share your X-treme dream.

Once upon a time, a young boy and his classmates were asked to write an essay about what they'd like to be and do when they grew up. The boy went home and wrote down his dream: he wanted to train horses on his own ranch. The next day, he turned in his report to his teacher.

When the assignment was handed back to him with an "F" grade he was bewildered. Not only did he receive an "F," he also received a request from the teacher to rewrite the assignment according to what the teacher thought was a more attainable goal. He believed the boy's dream was too impossible for him to achieve!

The boy went home and discussed the matter with his father. His father said he'd back his son either way he chose to go. If he didn't rewrite the assignment, he'd keep the "F." If he rewrote it, he stood a better chance of raising his grade.

The boy thought about it and decided not to rewrite the assignment. His X-treme dream for owning a large horse ranch remained in his heart until it became a reality when he grew up.

Every year, that same teacher brings other students out to visit the very ranch he told the young boy he'd never have. The teacher was proved wrong.

Who was that boy? Monty Roberts, the world-famous horse whisperer — on whom "The Horse Whisperer" movie is based.

You must never let anyone define for you who or what you'll be! Only the Lord is qualified to define that, because He made you and He has already designed you for greatness.

Thousands of years ago, another young boy named Joseph had several dreams given to him by the Lord God. Joseph was the favorite son of Jacob, one of Israel's great patriarchs. Joseph was just 17 years old when he began to have dreams that would forever change his life (Genesis 37:2-5).

Joseph decided to share his dreams with his older brothers. But, because of all the favor Joseph had with their father, the brothers hated Joseph. The sort of dreams he had to share only made matters worse.

Each dream seemed to say that Joseph would one day reign over his brothers and it made them hate him more (Genesis 37:8).

Joseph's brothers were so envious of him that they became his naysayers. As time went on, however, we see that Joseph's dreams did indeed come to pass and God restored his relationship with his brothers (Genesis 45:15). The fulfillment of his dreams saved his entire household and the future lineage of Israel.

Joseph persevered toward his dreams in spite of many perilous years away from his family while on the road to fulfillment of his X-treme dream. He never took his eyes off the dreams the Lord gave him, and he focused on them instead of the jealous words and acts of his brothers. God raised up Joseph to be a blessing and not a curse. You, too, can be just as victorious over your naysayers and dream-stealers!

I love Joseph's story because, through it, God teaches us the importance of wisely choosing who to share our dreams with, when to share them and how to deal with any possible naysayers. It is a true story of triumph over acts meant for evil, which the Lord used for His good purposes and the preservation of a nation.

You and the Lord have already begun to write your true-life story of victory and triumph. If you'd like to see what's going to happen next, read on!

Road Sign #3: Distractions from Various Sources

This is such a key road sign because of its subtlety. It can come from your friends, family, worthy causes and significant others. Staying on track with your vision is a must and you must keep all of your activities and how you spend your time in proper perspective. Choose to walk wisely without wavering in your vision.

JAMES 1:6B-8

Who wavers (hesitates, doubts) is like the billowing surge out at sea that is blown hither and thither and tossed by the wind. For truly, let not such a person imagine that he will receive anything [he asks for] from the Lord. [For being as he is] a man of two minds (hesitating, dubious, irresolute), [he is] unstable and unreliable and uncertain about everything [he thinks, feels, decides].

You must decide now to be aware of the fact that the enemy of our souls is constantly seeking out ways that he can bring something enticing to you that will trip you up and keep you from stepping into the reality of your dreams and vision for your life. Let no one or any thing distract you from what God has designed you to be and do!

While the nation of Israel was at war and King David was the commander-in-chief, he got distracted and decided to take a rest from the war. He chose to stay at his palace and while spending time on the roof, he spied a lovely woman named Bathsheba who was bathing (2 Samuel 11:1-3). He should have been fighting with his men but ended up coveting another man's wife. His distraction with Bathsheba caused him to plan the death of her husband Uriah and claim Bathsheba for his own. Later when Bathsheba conceived a child for King David, the child was lost as well. Two lives were lost over one distraction.

When Jesus came to the home of two sisters named Mary and Martha, we see Martha being busy serving Jesus and wondering why her sister is just sitting at His feet, hanging on His every word (Luke 10:39-40). Scripture tells us that Martha was 'distracted' with much serving. Here is an example of how worthy activities can even deter us from doing what is right. Jesus, the Son of God was in Martha's home but she was too busy to relish just being in His presence! If we keep our eyes on Him, He promises to take care of our worldly worries (Matthew 6:25-34). Uncompromising focus on God's individual vision for you is so key to your success.

Road Sign #4: Dissatisfaction with your Status Quo

At this stage of your journey, you are probably somewhat eager to see some real change in your life. I'm not surprised; it's to be expected. That sort of discomfort is allowing you to make room for the "new" season of life the Lord and you are progressing toward.

In other words, what used to be satisfying to you may not be now. The Lord is causing you to get out of your comfort zone. Are you feeling cramped where you are? Listen to:

Psalm 18:19

He brought me forth also into a large place. He was delivering me because He was pleased with me and delighted in me.

We must let go of the old in order to grab hold of the new. Don't be afraid of the feeling. Accept it and keep on walking down the road to your X-treme dream. God has freedom and so much more in store for you!

Road Sign #5: Hunger for God's Presence and Visionaries

Got a favorite food? One of my favorite treats is ice cream. I can eat it any time, any place and in any season of the year. It makes no difference to me. I thoroughly enjoy it. Sometimes I even get intense hankerings or a true hunger for it.

You're going to get intense hunger pains just like these for the Lord's presence. It will be like nothing you've ever felt before, because you are walking toward your destiny!

King David knew all too well what this hunger was like. He wrote the words for a very popular Christian chorus to describe his hunger pains in

Psalm 42:1-2

As the deer pants for streams of water, so my soul pants for you, O God. My soul thirsts for God, for the living God. When can I go and meet with God?

That gives such a graphic image of hunger and thirst, doesn't it? His desire for God's presence was very deep. Yours will be, too.

Are you sensing a desire or need to be around certain visionary people? Again, don't be surprised. Just go with the flow and ask the Lord what you are supposed to learn from the amazing saints He is about to put in your path. When it happens, just go with the flow. God will cause people you never knew before to **supernaturally** come to you. These people will be key to the realization of your X-treme dream.

Take a look at what the Lord did to bring the prophets Elijah and Elisha together in 1 Kings 19. First, the Lord spoke to Elijah in a still, small voice (verse 12), and then He told Elijah who to anoint as his successor and where to find him. God wanted Elisha to be servant to and successor of Elijah. What was the purpose of this holy alliance? The complete destruction of all child-sacrificing Baal worship in Israel. Is that awesome or what?

The story is not finished yet. If you keep reading in 2 Kings 2, you'll see that Elisha had a hunger to be in the presence of his mentor and fellow visionary, Elijah. **He refused to leave Elijah's presence**. And because of that hunger, Elisha was richly rewarded. Elisha desired a double portion of the prophetic anointing Elijah had. Because he clung to Elijah like a magnet, he was there to see the Lord catch his mentor up into heaven. And as promised, Elisha did receive the double-portion prophetic anointing (2 Kings 2:9-15).

This is not to be taken lightly, but with *expectancy*. You can count on it! It will happen. Look for it! You will become a "people magnet" for God's purposes.

Road Sign #6: Prophetic Dreams, Visions and Words

As soon as Shaunya and I decided to begin the X-treme dream journey to develop our film company, she began to have prophetic dreams. Our favorite is the one she had in 1995 that I recorded in my dream journal. (Any dream you have that stays with you long after you have it should probably be recorded for future reference. If you don't have a journal for recording visionary and/or prophetic things, *get one*! You must keep track of all that God does on your X-treme dream journey, because you'll have victories to rehearse in times of peril from which you can draw strength later.)

Shaunya dreamed that she had opened up a slick, four-color magazine to the "People To Watch" section and realized that it featured the two of us. The title of the article was "Sister Act." She felt strange about the dream because, at the time, we also had two male friends working with us at our company, but the article in the dream said nothing about the guys. Shaunya woke up wondering what it all meant and why the two men were not included in the story.

I wrote down all that she said. Once it was recorded, we didn't dwell on it; we just gave the dream back to the Lord and went on with our lives.

Two years later, in 1997, I was sitting at my desk in the news office where I worked when my phone rang. It was the associate editor for *Colorado Homes and Lifestyles.* She had heard about my sister and I and wanted to know if we'd be interested in doing an interview for her magazine. The Denver media had already done several stories on us, but we'd never done an interview for this magazine.

Sweat began to run down my arms when the editor went on to say that she wanted to place the feature on us in the "People To Watch" section. She also said they had already decided to title our story "Sister Act." I nearly dropped the phone! What also matched the dream in 1995 was the fact that both of our male friends had moved away and were no longer working with us! The icing on our "dream" cake was that *Colorado Homes and Lifestyles* is a slick, four-color magazine-just like the magazine Shaunya saw in her dream!

Our dream article appeared in the November/December 1997 issue. Shaunya's dream had foretold something that was yet to come. This is important to note: *if we had not recorded the dream when it happened,* we might have missed this supernatural occurrence.

Get ready to receive prophetic dreams, visions and words spoken by prophetic people during your life. Put your faith out there and remember that faith is the substance of things hoped for and the evidence of things unseen (Hebrews 11:1). God breathes life into things that are born in the prophetic realm of the supernatural. Pictures and words you'll see and hear with this road sign are waiting to manifest in your natural life.

Road Sign #7: Divine Appointments

When you see this road sign, you are rolling along on the favor of God in a most unusual way. It is here that God supernaturally puts you before the so-called "great men" of this world that King Solomon refers to in Proverbs 18:16. These are divine appointments.

What makes an appointment divine? The fact that God schedules them without your knowing it. There is an amazing planning book in the heavenly realm with your name on it. God systematically sets up connections that coincide with distinct moments so you can see His hand bringing about His divine purpose and destiny for your life.

God prepares you and places you right in front of the very people who will set your X-treme dream ball in motion. You'll know it when it happens because you'll see quite clearly that it could not have happened except by the miraculous, wonder-working power of God.

There is an exciting example of this scheduling found in the Book of Esther. Esther is a star in God's book, which is exactly what her name means. She was a young, orphaned Jewess raised by her cousin Mordecai (Esther 2:7). After the King of Persia divorced his wife, he held a sort of beauty pageant to replace her. Through a series of events, arranged by God, Esther found favor in his sight and became his new queen (Esther 2:17).

The Lord is eager to do the same kind of planning for you when you choose to walk out your X-treme dream in partnership with Him. Imagine being an orphan one day and queen of an entire empire the next! True story. God is waiting to write your amazing, true story.

I've seen the Lord's appointments on numerous occasions to accomplish His will in my life. When my sister and I needed a favor in Hollywood, God caused me to be placed in the same room with an A-list producer who I had long admired. I was prepared spiritually and professionally for that divine appointment because I had done all the Lord's voice and all that my A-Team had instructed me to do! I had been encouraged to fast and pray before the trip and be myself. Another admonishment from my team was not to dilute the strength of the words God had given me to speak to my illustrious film industry colleagues. It was the start of a great friendship with one of the most influential Christians in Hollywood. Now Shaunya and I are personally acquainted with him.

Do you ever wonder how to handle your fear or what to say in certain circumstances? Remember the words of encouragement God spoke to Jeremiah:

Jeremiah 1:5, 7-9

Before I formed you in the womb I knew and approved of you as My chosen instrument, and before you were born I separated and set you apart, consecrat-

ing you; [and] I appointed you as a prophet to the nations. But the Lord said to me, Say not, I am only a youth; for you shall go to all whom I shall send you, and whatever I command you, you shall speak. Be not afraid of them [their faces], for I am with you to deliver you, says the Lord. Then the Lord put forth His hand and touched my mouth. And the Lord said to me, Behold, I have put My words in your mouth.

God promises to actively perform His word in Verse 12 of the same chapter.

It just doesn't get any better than this! God's word is pure gold that you can take to the bank. Our God is no respecter of persons, meaning He doesn't play favorites. What He did for me and Jeremiah, He will most certainly do for you!

Road Sign #8: Divine Conversations

Sometimes you can have a great need for certain words or a special message of some sort along the way. Do you realize that you just might be one conversation away from greatness?

God's plan involves more than just being next to the right person at the right time. Your speech can be divinely ordered or inspired so that His will is brought to fulfillment through one or more conversations. That's right. One conversation can be the catalyst to your grabbing the world by the tail and swinging it over your head. Or, talking to the right person at the right time can cause the other person to soar. You and the Lord win in both situations.

Times like these are electric. God will divinely give you the words to speed up the vision and the production of its fruit. The Apostle Philip had some wild encounters that are recorded in the Book of Acts. One of my favorite stories takes place in Acts 8:26-39 and involves his divine conversation with an Ethiopian eunuch.

Now an angel of the Lord said to Philip, "Go south to the road—the desert road — that goes down from Jerusalem to Gaza." So he started out, and on his way he met an Ethiopian eunuch, an important official in charge of all the treasury of Candace, queen of the Ethiopians. This man had gone to

Jerusalem to worship, and on his way home was sitting in his chariot reading the book of Isaiah the prophet. The Spirit told Philip, "Go to that chariot and stay near it." Then Philip ran up to the chariot and heard the man reading Isaiah the prophet.

"Do you understand what you are reading?," Philip asked. "How can I?" he said, "unless someone explains it to me?" So he invited Philip to come up and sit with him. The eunuch was reading this passage of Scripture:

He was led like a sheep to the slaughter,
and as a lamb before the shearer is silent,
so he did not open his mouth. In his
humiliation he was deprived of justice.
Who can speak of his descendants?
For his life was taken from the earth.

The eunuch asked Philip, "Tell me please, who is the prophet talking about, himself or someone else?" Then Philip began with that very passage of Scripture and told him the good news about Jesus. As they traveled along the road, they came to some water and the eunuch said, "Look, here is water. Why shouldn't I be baptized?" And he gave orders to stop the chariot. Then both Philip and the eunuch went down into the water and Philip baptized him. When they came up out of the water, the Spirit of the Lord suddenly took Philip away, and the eunuch did not see him again, but went on his way rejoicing.

On a trip to Hollywood, Shaunya and I were contacted by a millionaire who wanted to have dinner with us. The gentleman and his assistant had come from England, and I wondered what the Lord wanted to do during our dinner meeting.

During dinner, I discovered that the businessman had recently met a very influential man in the film industry earlier that week. He told me that he wanted to send a thank-you letter to the man but didn't know what to say.

Instantly the Lord gave me the words for the thank-you letter. That one conversation was why the Lord caused the dinner to take place! It had nothing to do with the restaurant or what we ate at all. It was all about the words that God caused me to speak to this British businessman.

As a result of the success of that conversation, my sister and I were later invited to England for a special dinner, in our honor, at the millionaire's estate. Another wonderful friendship was started because of the supernatural workings of the Holy Spirit, just like in Philip's story.

When you make a conscious decision to partner with the Lord throughout all your travels toward the dream, He will meet you there. He will provide the words to speak and the necessary wisdom. **Put your confidence in Him and His ability!** You'll never go wrong.

Road Sign #9: Divine Opportunities

I call opportunities "open doors" and, again, only God can cause them. Open doors can suddenly appear when you need a job or need to go someplace where God has need of you. Open doors change the course of your life in an exciting way. Open doors cause you to make decisions you've never had to make before as well. Usually those decisions are for new things in your life. Once you walk through one of these open doors, you give yourself the chance to move closer to the goals of your vision or X-treme dream.

The key to divine opportunities is your ability to be still and let God be God as you wait for Him to show you the next move. Sometimes it's as simple as making do with what the Lord has already given you. You could be smack dab in the middle of a real uncertainty and God will come to open your new door.

When I was an editor for a national food magazine, the company decided to move to Washington, D.C. The publisher wanted me to relocate with everyone else on the staff, but the Lord was telling me to hold on and not make the move.

Everyone started taking trips to D.C. to find their new apartments and get acquainted with our nation's capital. I couldn't participate because God had already told me to be still. Did I know what my new post would be? I hadn't the slightest idea.

I only knew one thing: Whenever I'd needed money before, the Lord had allowed me to do some catering. I decided to use what He'd shown me to do with my hands and start catering again.

While I was finishing up the last couple of magazine issues for the Denver office, a woman called to say she'd heard about my cooking and wondered if I'd like to cater her Christmas party. I said yes and we set a date.

The party was a huge success. Recognition as a caterer felt great, but I wondered how long I might be catering before the Lord allowed me to go back to using my journalism skills full-time. It didn't take long for God to make a move.

As I put the woman's kitchen back in order after the party, her husband returned home from a business trip. Over a slice of my cherry cheesecake, he introduced himself to me as "Jack" and began to ask me all sorts of questions about myself. It felt like a job interview. But how could it be? I hardly knew these people.

Jack kept on grilling me about my career vision and went to his study to bring me a job application from the place where he worked. I was shocked! How many husbands offer jobs to caterers they hardly know in their kitchens? God was clearly at work here! He is often very sneaky. I read the application and promised to call Jack's contact in the public affairs office. **This was my open door!**

Four months after the party at his house, I was hired as a news officer at the U.S. Environmental Protection Agency (EPA) where Jack worked.

My job was full of surprises. You see, Jack had never really told me what he did for the EPA. He had only said he was a manager of sorts. That's all I knew. I found out the first day that Jack was a manager all right. He was the number two guy in charge of environmental protection at the federal level for six states in the Rocky Mountain West! I was later told that Jack is the most decorated person in civil service alive today. God had seen to it that a "great man" in the federal government would roll out the red carpet for me — his daughter, Princess Charlynne. I was overjoyed!

God's love and care for you and I runs very deep. Each of you is either a prince or a princess of the Most High God. His word says so, because we are all joint heirs with Christ in His eternal kingdom

(Romans 8:16-17). Are you excited yet? You should be! It's time to reveal the last road sign.

Road Sign #10: Witty Inventions

Has God ever given you a new or witty invention? He is the Master of all creativity and has gifted many of His human creations with the ability to create wondrous things to further His purposes.

PROVERBS 8:12 KING JAMES VERSION

I wisdom, dwell with prudence, and find out knowledge of witty inventions.

Along the path of your X-treme dream, you will more than likely need a witty invention or idea to spur you on toward the completion of your destiny. These inventions and ideas can come in all shapes and sizes. You and I serve a fathomless God who is full of inventions and ideas never seen or heard of before. These ideas are not gender-based either. **Princes and princesses can get witty inventions.**

My friend Donna Auguste made the "Fortune 500" list in 2001 with the witty invention God gave her through the software company He inspired her to start. She is a young engineer who currently holds all the patents on the technology that brought us the Palm Pilot.

Donna's long-term vision or X-treme dream was to create a non-profit organization that would allow her to bring medicine, education and communications technology to the rural villages of Kenya and Tanzania. The witty invention God gave Donna, the technology used for the Palm Pilot, was the beginning of her journey. And when the Lord told her to sell her company, she did it.

The profits from the sale allowed her to open the Leave a Little Room Foundation to fund her overseas efforts. She has also started an Internet gospel music station and store that marries her love of God and her love of gospel music. Donna is just beginning the rest of her X-treme dream lifestyle. She trusted God with His word and watched Him perform marvelous things!

In a previous chapter I shared with you the story of the creation of my oatmeal cookies in college. That is yet another example of a witty invention God gave me to further His purposes. While the cookies themselves were great, the purpose for them went deeper than taste and gastronomic satisfaction. God caused me to create a cookie recipe so that two young girls (Charlynne and Julie Mong) could have the funds necessary to go to England to further the spread of the Gospel. That trip was a pivotal point in both of our lives and one we'll never forget. Over the years, God has used me and my cooking in so many ways to bring about His divine plan. When God says, "Cook," I do it, because He always has something cooking behind the scenes, and seasoning my cooking with adventure is usually part of His plan. It's exciting to me because I never know where God will send me with my catering creations.

Got any ideas swirling around in your head? Take a moment to write some of them down here if you haven't already done so on your Vision Grid.

Witty Inventions on the Burner

1. ______________________________
2. ______________________________
3. ______________________________
4. ______________________________
5. ______________________________
6. ______________________________
7. ______________________________

Now turn the thoughts and plans for these ideas over to the Lord. Wait for His lead on what your next step will be. He'll never steer you wrong! And, whatever you do, *keep your expectancy alive*! Any and every thing is possible for you. Believe it! Live this truth!

CHAPTER 9

X-TREMELY SINGULAR: A MESSAGE FOR SINGLES

I am personally convinced that one person can be a change catalyst,
a "transformer" in any situation, any organization.
Such an individual is yeast that can leaven an entire loaf . . .
— STEPHEN R. COVEY

Be spiritually accountable to your friends and stay involved
in the spiritual community that is responsible for your growth.
— DRS. HENRY CLOUD & JOHN TOWNSEND

I don't know the key to success,
but the key to failure is to try to please everybody.
— BILL COSBY

My desire is to have you free from all anxiety and distressing care.
The unmarried man is anxious about the things of the Lord —
how he may please the Lord. And the unmarried woman or girl
is concerned and anxious about the matters of the Lord —
how to be wholly separated and set apart in body and spirit . . .
— THE APOSTLE PAUL IN 1 CORINTHIANS 7:32,34

Unanswered petitions are not unheard.
They are treasured in the King's archives.
— OSWALD CHAMBERS

My reasons for including this chapter are many, but the main one is this: If you are a single person, you MUST get a proper understanding of the strength, power and authority you possess in your singleness. I, too, want you to be free from anxiety and distress on your journey, just like the Apostle Paul. Your years as a single person can, and should, be some of the most fulfilling of your life because of the very reasons Paul stated in 1 Corinthians 7.

I am 37 years old and have yet to be married or have children. Believe it or not, I have turned down three, yes three, marriage proposals to some very special and talented Christian men.

Do I want to be married? Yes, but not at the risk of jeopardizing God's perfect will for the X-treme dream He has designed for my future mate and I. I believe it is not okay to marry just anyone; I believe we have a responsibility to marry the *right* Christian person. Our individual X-treme dreams are too precious to the Lord for us to do anything but that.

Some of you may choose to be celibate until Christ's return. That's terrific if that's what you hear the Lord telling you to do. I send blessings to you as you do it. My own mother was only married once, and when my father divorced her, she chose a life of celibacy — for over 23 years now. Sounds impossible in this day and age, but it can be done.

Most of you probably want to be married someday. I'm with you on that and feel I would be remiss in writing a book about vision without sharing with you some truths on the dynamics for singles and couples who want to live a lifestyle of X-treme proportions. Both marital states are blessed by God, and yet they have some strong differences. As you will discover as you start your X-treme dream process, each marital status has blessings and challenges.

I am going to share with you some personal anecdotes from my life and the lives of others that I hope will be helpful to you. Together, we'll take a hard look at choices and decisions offered to us all along the way as single dreamers.

This chapter is going to ask you to look at choices you've made in your life so far. The Lord has not created us to be robots, but rather creatures of free will. That means you and I get to make decisions for our lives every day, with or without God's help.

The main question is this: How many times have you consciously made decisions based on your vision? Have you ever made a decision based on the vision God designed for your life? Good decisions bring fruit to your life; bad decisions bring destruction to your dreams and vision. Take a minute or two to jot down some good decisions and then some not-so-good decisions.

Good Decisions

1. ______________________________
2. ______________________________
3. ______________________________
4. ______________________________
5. ______________________________

Bad Decisions

1. ______________________________
2. ______________________________
3. ______________________________
4. ______________________________
5. ______________________________

These notes may include actions you took in high school or college, people you dated, subjects you chose to study, items you bought, words you spoke, etc. You've had a chance in the previous chapters to see God's original blueprint for your life. It should be easier to see now how your choices over the years have affected your vision and destiny. The best thing to remember after doing this exercise is that God is in the redemption business. **He can redeem anything and anyone.** Nothing is too difficult for Him! He promises this in

JEREMIAH 32:17, 27

Alas, Lord God! Behold, You have made the heavens and the earth by Your great power and by Your outstretched arm! There is nothing too hard or too wonderful for You. Behold, I am the Lord, the God of all flesh; is there anything too hard for Me?

It's never too late to get back on the right track with Him. But it's even better to never get derailed in the first place. I want to help you see how to do that in this chapter.

Sometimes we make wrong decisions because we don't have a clear picture of who we are in Jesus and what kind of authority we have in Him. If you knew you had a royal title in a special kingdom, wouldn't you want to act like it? Well, guess what, you **are** royalty! You do have a title and God sees you seated with Him in heavenly places. Want a glimpse of what God says about your authority?

You are called to walk as kings, given all authority and all power over the enemy. The enemy fears you, and he fears that you might understand who you are, and that you might rise to that occasion and bring forth the slingshot even as David did, and with a heartfelt cry of "Is there not a cause?" My cause will become your cause, says the Lord, and when My cause becomes yours, then the giants of this land will fall.

That is a portion of a prophetic message spoken at Faith Tabernacle in Kremmling, Colorado on April 7, 2002. The words are appropriate for all of us because it is easy to downplay our spiritual authority in God. It was the power of one that slew Goliath.

You must grasp the importance of your life, fully submitted to the Lord, as a single person. The enemy of your soul would love for you to miss this principle and distract you from ever becoming what your blueprint from God says you are.

Let me tell you this: Satan and his cohorts will not be sending you something that is obviously evil to distract you. No sirree! He will try to entice you with things like getting married to someone before you or your spouse-to-be are ready. The "blueprint spoiler" can come in the packaging or disguise of a "nice" Christian man or woman who is the ultimate **counterfeit** for the person God planned to be your mate . . . before you were even born! This sort of evil can deter you from walking out the destiny and fulfilling the purpose God specifically designed for you **and** the other person.

Marrying the wrong person at the wrong time is one of the biggest threats to singles with a vision or X-treme dream brewing in their spirits. God has given you all the resources to make wise decisions at each step of the journey. There is no need to make hasty decisions. Let's make the right choices for the right reasons.

Seek to have a spotless testimony in this important area of your life. God will definitely honor you because of it. You have a choice to make the right decision regarding your future and your mate. Let the Lord guide you, and when you hear that still, small voice, obey it! It will save you years of anguish and regret down the road.

Someone I met with recently told me they decided to get married because they lost their vision. Ouch! I don't think that guy's new bride would enjoy hearing that she was the consolation prize because her new hubbie lost his dream. That would be a nightmare.

I am stressing this because marriage and your vision are not a game! Having no vision is a poor motivator for marrying someone. Two fragmented people don't make a whole marriage. Single men, you should be seeking God's face for your vision if you want to be the spiritual leader of your home someday. Single women, you should let God lead you to the godly man who has a vision and an X-treme dream that complements the X-treme dream God has already given you. A man without a vision will die inwardly. Why entrust your life to a person who is blindly leading you to some unknown destination? You've heard the old saying that, if you don't have a map, then any destination will do. If you wander in the wilderness without a compass, you may spend your entire life lost to God's dream for you.

Remember what I said in a previous chapter. You are not a threat to the enemy if you don't know your vision or purpose. The minute you realize who you are in Jesus, you can crush Satan's head!

Let's be singles with purpose who impact the world we've been given in a radical, history-making way! While God is preparing your character and the character of your future spouse for marriage, be busy living the life God has given you in the largest way you can. Yes, live large! Make each day count! Carpe diem!

Are you tired of waiting for Mister or Miss Right? I know that times are hard for singles everywhere in the globe and that it seems like your time is slow in coming. Your Heavenly Father sees and hears you. He is not on vacation where you are concerned.

At various times in my singleness, I've cried out, "Are you there, God? It's me, Charlynne." God has answered me in some amazing ways. He used many of His anointed saints to speak to me. In March 1991, God spoke through a missionary from Africa who I hadn't seen since 1980. These are some of the words she said to me about my future mate: ". . . There might be one or two men who you think might be 'the one' and you'll want to move, but don't do that. You're gonna wait for God's plan and it's gonna work for His glory and you're gonna see God say, 'I chose for you the right person in the right hour."

There were two men in my life at that time who I thought could be right for me, and yet I knew God was saying "No" on both counts because of my vision. The missionary came to confirm what the Holy Spirit had already told me. God didn't want me to stumble in any way during my season of waiting.

And again, in October 1997, an Albuquerque businesswoman spoke to me about my mate and the call on my life: "God wanted me to be married before He established me in my ministry. But to you, He says that He wants to establish you in ministry first before being married."

Those words were also confirmation of messages the Lord had already spoken to my heart. That means that ALL of my decisions needed to coincide with the voice of the Lord. As I grew older, I wondered if this word would stay. When I received my minister's license, I realized that the ministry was evidence of that word. I am now a recognized minister of the Gospel, called to be an evangelist, and yet I wear no one's ring. God indeed established me as a curate before I became someone's wife or mother.

I shared those words of encouragement from my own life to tell you that God will move heaven and earth to get a message of such importance through to you. If He could use a whale to get to Jonah, He can speak to you at critical times about decisions regarding the course of your life and who you should marry.

You can't afford to make choices rashly and without God's wisdom or peace. It can mean the difference between your living a life of divine purpose or living in mediocrity. And here's the clincher: Choices you make regarding your mate will directly affect your children for good or bad and for generations to come. This is serious business folks! **God does not have to pay for something He has not ordered for our lives.** We must learn how to rightly apply His wisdom to the decisions we face. **Wisdom is the principal thing** (Proverbs 4:7)!

I also want you to know that these truths apply to **every** part of your life. Every decision or choice you make should be based on what the Lord is saying to you about your purpose and destiny. If you make decisions in piecemeal fashion, you will reap what God has prepared for you in piecemeal fashion. I know you want *all* God has stored up for you, and you want *all* God has marked with your name on it. Right? Right! So let's apply His truths and wisdom to every area of our lives, not just those areas that are covenient and easy for us. **Say no to every counterfeit offer from the enemy's camp!** You can do it!

Now I want to tell you a true story about an individual who was extremely gifted by the Lord in the realm of acting. Her name is Danielle.

She had a vision to go as high as she could with her acting and had a call on her life to impact the secular world with her special talents. Throughout her growing-up years, God sent several prophetic people to speak into her life about all the fantastic things He had prepared for her if she obeyed His voice and leading in every area of her life. Some of the people were famous evangelists and some were unknown, but all of the words they spoke were confirmation that God had big things for her to do in the Kingdom.

As Danielle entered her 30s, she realized that most of her friends were married, and she began to get anxious about her singleness. She decided to date anyone she could, in hopes of meeting Mr. Right. Danielle got herself into some pretty dangerous situations spiritually and physically. During this time, she asked godly people for advice but shunned their words of wisdom because what they told her did not tickle her ears.

Danielle even began to have vivid dreams about her situation. In those dreams, God clearly told her not to proceed with her self-inflicted "search and destroy" mission. She refused His warnings. (Sometimes God will send you messages when you're asleep because He can't get you to listen to His still, small voice when you're awake.) She also refused the advice of her mentors and closest friends.

By this time, Danielle was exclusively dating a man who had a questionable background. He was a Christian who attended her church, but he also made sure that Danielle severed all ties with her family and friends.

Right at the time Danielle decided to let this man take over her life, the divine opportunity or open door she'd waited for her entire life was presented to her. A Christian organization decided to back her acting group, and they were offered a contract that would have allowed all of them to quit their 9-to-5 jobs and follow their acting visions. It was everything that God had promised her and more!

Within about 90 days of signing the big deal, Danielle was caught in a sexually compromising position with her new beau. Bad news often travels fast and, because of that ungodly circumstance, the Christian backers retracted the contract. Soon after that, Danielle dissolved her relationship with everyone in her group. A few months later, she married the man who helped her into that compromising position.

To this day, Danielle has never regained the place she had in her acting vision, and her vision of reaching the lost in the secular world of acting was severely destroyed. Now she's married with three children and is out of touch with every person in her family and all of her old acting partners.

It's important to note that Danielle didn't get into sexual sin with a non-Christian, but with a Bible college graduate. Sin can happen in the church as well as outside of it. **The enemy is playing hardball these days! Listen up, because he is a crafty adversary.** Anything Satan can do to rob you of true fulfillment in Christ, he will. He is very subtle. In this true story, he used a Christian against another Christian, which is not uncommon. **Make sure something like this doesn't happen to you.**

As possible as it is to blow it and end up in a relationship that is not God's best for you, it's just as easy to hear His voice and become everything He designed you to be.

There is a young woman I know very well. She is my sister, business partner and only sibling. I'm talking about Shaunya.

Earlier I told you that I had turned down three offers of marriage. My sister Shaunya has turned down two.

Sound strange? It really isn't. You see, we are members of each other's A-Teams and we've vowed to keep each other in check with regard to our X-treme dreams and any potential mate who could come on the scene. We know that the decision for a mate is potentially the most important decision a single person can make, for or against his or her vision. We are committed to living the X-treme dream as a lifestyle on a daily basis and holding each other accountable in the process. My sister and I have made a decision to live out our visions before the Lord and we'll only accept His best and those things that pertain to the vision.

Shaunya went to Oral Roberts University as an English major, with a deep desire to work as a screenwriter when she graduated. She also wanted to give back to young people in the midst of pursuing her dream. During that time, a great guy talked with her about his intentions for their future together, but she felt the timing was not right. So they remained friends and she went on with her life, staying focused on her vision at all times.

A year later, another great Christian guy came forward. They had a good friendship, and then one day it became apparent by his words and actions that he wanted a life with her. Shaunya knew that his vision and hers did not complement each other, but he didn't care. He knew he wanted her in his life and didn't care that their visions were at opposite ends of the spectrum. Shaunya knew it would never work and politely refused his offer.

As a result of Shaunya's sticking to her guns, she has become an influential writer and director with valuable relationships from Hollywood to London. She is a respected mentor to young women and a beloved and active godmother to four small children.

Does she ever want to get married? Shaunya is not opposed to the idea, but she will never compromise her God-given vision just to wear a ring and become Mrs. Somebody. In short, Shaunya is quite content in her life as a single writer/director. She is a whole person in her Lord and Savior Jesus Christ.

When folks ask 34-year-old Shaunya what she's doing in the guy department, she says, "I'm working on being findable." She is actively building her character while she waits on the Lord and serves His purposes. She is NOT plotting and scheming about how to catch a man.

Scripture tells us in Proverbs 18:22 that a man is the one who finds a wife. Both of us want to be found by the man of God's own choosing for us. It will save us tons of heartache and regret down the road. And we have no regrets of any kind in the choices we've made. Our lives are truly blessed — a living, breathing testimony of the power of vision in the lives of Christian women. We believe that the treasure we hold on the inside of us is only to be shared with the mate the Lord brings to us.

In the meantime, we lead full, exciting, adventuresome lives as single women sold out to Jesus and loving every minute of our X-treme dreams. You can, too!

Here are seven fireproof words of wisdom (WOWs) for all you singles out there. Each one has served me well during my wait for the godly warrior and partner who will walk with me through our X-treme dreams.

WOWs for Singles

1. Make sure your #1 relationship is with your first love — Jesus Christ. Date Him more than anyone else. When you put Him first, He promises to give you the desires of your heart. Yes, even those secret petitions you may not have shared with anyone but Him (Psalm 37:4).

2. Got wisdom? No? Then get it! Remember, it's the principal thing. In times of uncertainty, seek to please the Lord instead of everyone else.

3. Get an A-Team. You must have accountability as a single man or woman. Remember that the A-Team is not only to give you advice but also prayer cover. Someone besides you should be watching your back.

4. Guard your heart and mind (Philippians 4:7). This will bring you peace no matter what stage of life you're in. Watch who you spend time with and what you put into your mind. Singles are particularly vulnerable in this area.

5. Check out all — not some — decisions with the Lord first, and then with your A-Team. Make sure that all of your critical decisions line up with the original blueprint — your purpose and destiny — according to the Lord's plan for you. Stay close to your true friends. Never shun an old friend who loves you because you think Mister or Miss Right is knocking on your door. You will always need your friends, single or married.

6. If and when marriage is presented to you, pray hard, listen for the still, small voice of the Lord and vow to obey it no matter what. Never, ever choose your flesh over the voice of the Holy Spirit.

7. Complete the X-treme dream exercises and homework outlined in this book. They are especially designed to help you become more intimate with your Lord and yourself. Taken seriously, this course of action can totally change your life in a miraculous way with everlasting results.

Finally, single men and women, enjoy your time of freedom to be and do *all* God designed you to be and do. Relish this time in your life because, chances are, you will not always have it. This season of singleness is a blessed gift. Use it well and *live large* as you wait for the next season to begin. God loves you very much and has nothing but your best interests at heart. He knows you and your needs better than you know yourself, because He made you.

Here's one more message I'd like to share that I received from the Lord as a freshman in college. I pray that it blesses you as much as it has me over the years. This is for every single person in Christ who is waiting for their mate. The year was 1984 and I was at Oral Roberts University, in Tulsa, Oklahoma.

To My Single Sons and Daughters —

Everyone longs to give themselves completely to someone, to have a deep, soul relationship with another, to be loved thoroughly and exclusively. But God says to a Christian, "No, not until you are satisfied, fulfilled and content with being loved by me alone, with giving yourself totally and unreservedly to Me, to having an intensely personal and unique relationship with Me alone, discovering that only in Me is your satisfaction to be found. Only then will you be capable of the perfect human relationship I have planned for you. You will never be united with another until you are united with Me, exclusive of anyone or anything else, exclusive of any other desires or longings.

I want you to stop planning, stop wishing, and allow Me to bring it to you. You just keep watching Me, expecting the greatest things. Keep experiencing the satisfaction that I AM. Keep listening and learning the things I tell you. You just wait. That's all.

Don't be anxious. Don't worry. Don't look around at the things others have gotten or that I've given them. Don't look at the things you think you want. You just keep looking off and away up to Me, or you will miss what I want to show you.

And then, when you are ready, I'll surprise you with a love far more wonderful than any you would dream of. You see, until you are ready and until the one I have for you is ready (I am working even this moment to have both of you ready at the same time), until you are both satisfied exclusively with Me and the life I have prepared for you, you won't be able to experience the love that exemplifies your relationship with Me and is thus the perfect love.

Dear one, I want you to have this most wonderful love. I want you to see in the flesh a picture of your everlasting union of beauty, perfection and love that I offer you with Myself. ***Know that I love you utterly. I AM. Believe and be satisfied.***

All My Love,
Your Heavenly Father

Now let's go on and chat about issues to consider for couples embarking on the X-treme journey. Their needs are different from those of singles.

CHAPTER 10

X-TREME COUPLES: DOUBLE DREAMING

Growing in oneness is a process.
— LINDA DILLOW & LORRAINE PINTUS

As the church is subject to Christ, so let wives also be subject in everything to their husbands.
— EPHESIANS 5:24

He who finds a [true] wife finds a good thing and obtains favor from the Lord.
— PROVERBS 18:22

But the married man is anxious about worldly matters — how he may please his wife — and he is drawn in diverging directions [his interests are divided and he is distracted from his devotions to God], but the married woman has her cares [centered] in earthly affairs — how she may please her husband.
— 1 CORINTHIANS 7:33, 34

Now that I've exhorted the singles, it's time to build up the couples. You all are just as special as the singles, but different. Instead of dealing with one dream, you as a couple have individual dreams plus the dream the Lord has created for you as a couple.

	1 whole person with vision
+	**1 whole person with vision**
	1 X-tremely great marriage under God

I recently had the chance to do an X-treme dream seminar for a couple with three kids. Both of the parents were excited to do this with me because they had never made a decision for themselves or their family based on God's vision or X-treme dream for them. If your circumstance is similar, keep reading. God can redeem the time, and He will if you decide to partner with Him right now as a couple, committed to His vision for you.

If you want to seek God for your X-treme dream as a couple but have not done an individual Vision Grid for the two of you, please stop and take the time to do it.

Sometimes the hardest thing to do is think as an individual in the process because you are so used to being "one." Couples doing this for the first time often find out glorious things about their partners that they never knew before. The tools in this book are designed to help individuals get a true picture of all God has put inside of you.

It's easy to lose sight of some of those things when you get married and start a family.

Stop for a moment and jot down some of the dreams and desires you have that are unfulfilled. God has so much for you individually and as a couple.

Dreams Yet to Come

1. ______________________________
2. ______________________________
3. ______________________________
4. ______________________________
5. ______________________________
6. ______________________________
7. ______________________________

It's important to do this even as a married person, because people usually have 50 million reasons why their dreams and visions can wait. Someone at a seminar told me that they would love to work on their vision when they whittled their responsibilities down! Folks, if you as a couple wait for that to happen, the vision will never materialize. God has a plan for bringing balance to your life right now so you can live out your X-treme dreams *now*, not someday!

Impossible, you say? All things are possible with God. Nothing is too difficult for Him. When we take one step at a time in our X-treme dream journey, He will bring the balance necessary to keep you in forward motion as individuals and as couples.

Every chapter in this book has true stories and tips to help you progress toward your vision until it becomes a reality. When you follow the process outlined in these pages, you will see that God's word is alive and well.

Once two people decide to marry, they become one, and yet they are also still individuals. God knows there are challenges to face when two people decide to build a life together. He is the One who created "family," who made it possible for people to live and grow together in unity. It is possible and totally God's will for couples to recognize the unique traits and talents of each spouse and still have a common vision for their household.

Whenever I lead X-treme dream seminars for couples, I walk them through the process of writing out their individual dreams, and then I bring the spouses together to discuss the vision for their household. Many couples end up hearing their other half's deepest desires for the first time. The exercises bring real honesty to the table. Couples often call and say that going through the process of dream-building together strengthened their marriage.

In Chapter Three I mentioned a couple with a blended family, Sue and Ben, who took the seminar with me. I love their story because of the challenges they faced and overcame. They are two very different individuals who are living victoriously with individual dreams and a united dream as a family.

I call couples like Sue and Ben "wonder couples." They walked through the same process outlined in this book and made a conscious decision to keep Jesus Christ at the center of their marriage and every individual and joint decision they made along the way. Being married doesn't mean that those secret petitions of your heart can't be fulfilled. God never says "this or the other" in a situation, but rather "you can have this *and* that." Remember, the possibilities are endless when it comes to Him and all He has stored up for us. He is the God of more than enough.

Now let's take a closer look at how the wonder couple began to walk out their X-treme dream. One of the first things I remember is that they were consistently **honest**. They did not hold back from each other what they really wanted to accomplish as people of vision.

When they came to the seminar, there was no physical evidence that what they dreamed would come true. This is when the Lord took His "super" abilities and matched them with the couple's "natural" abilities and gifts. All they had was the Lord and their talents as individuals.

As it turned out, that's all they needed. God always multiplies what we bring to Him in an **exponential** way. That's why He's the All-Sufficient One!

Sue and Ben also looked for opportunities to bless each other and others on their X-treme dream journey. When Sue was experiencing difficulties, Ben encouraged her to go away and spend time alone or with some of her special friends. One of Ben's favorite things to do was take long cross-country bike treks with their son. So when Ben needed a break from his hectic work schedule, Sue inspired him to go do it.

I have always advised people to help others while waiting for the realization of an X-treme dream. It is totally contrary to what the world might say, but it's wisdom. You simply cannot out-give God. Sue and Ben knew this and were not neglectful of the fact that there were things they could do to bless others while waiting in the wings for the fruition of their vision.

Celebrations for every member of the family are musts for this couple. When victories are looming on the horizon, they celebrate and enjoy praising God, and they make and relish time with each other. They often take trips together to have quality time as a couple and strategize for the next leg of their dream. God continues to bless them along the way.

He will do the same for you as you give Him your visions and keep Him at the center of your union. Every couple and their family has an opportunity to create their own special ways of showing love and celebrating their successes.

Ways to Celebrate as a Couple

1. ______________________________
2. ______________________________
3. ______________________________
4. ______________________________
5. ______________________________
6. ______________________________
7. ______________________________

I'd like to introduce another couple: Heather and Paul. I call them a wonder couple, too. Paul is a diplomat and Heather is a schoolteacher in the foreign country where they live.

When I first met this couple, I knew they were destined for greatness because of their consistent dedication to hearing God's still, small voice and then obeying it. The dynamics of this couple are totally different from Sue and Ben.

While Sue and Ben began the X-treme dream journey as a blended family in their 40s and in a second marriage, Heather and Paul were in their 30s and had no children at the start of their journey together. However, they have since adopted a teen from Thailand. Their story is a great one to point out, because they knew they were to be parents but didn't know how it was going to happen.

Heather and Paul are living their X-treme dream every day by choosing to recognize and celebrate the individual gifts in each other. They keep their focus on the overall vision God has given them as a couple and as new parents of a teenage daughter from a country other than their own. Paul and Heather also knew the Lord wanted to use Paul in the international business arena, but they didn't know that the Lord would open a door for him to work at a foreign embassy.

We have no idea how God will bring about His plans and purposes in our lives. It can be, and usually is, done in a way or timing you would never have chosen for yourself. His ways truly are higher than ours (Isaiah 55: 8-9). Hallelujah for that!

Your trust as a couple must be committed to the Lord. Trusting Him with your individual and joint visions and dreams is more important than anything else. Your visions are not dependent on yourselves, in the ways you might think. Your vision's outcome depends on how solid a partnership you and your partner have with the Lord.

The tool I use in this book to help you strategize with the Lord on your vision is the Vision Grid. It creates a visual picture for you as a couple to communicate to each other and to the Lord what He has already placed in your hearts.

When His will and yours are matched, the way before you is blessed and sure to become a reality.

Doing a grid first for yourselves as individuals and then jointly as a couple keeps both of you focused on what the Lord wants to do in you separately and through you as a couple. The grid is also a simple tool to use with others in your accountability circle. When used properly, it keeps the lines of communication open between you, the Lord and your team.

Why is all of this so important? Because the enemy loves to destroy families, and to do that, he will take aim at your marriage and try to muddy your vision. You must be fully aware of how dangerous you are when you operate within your God-designed purpose.

Nothing is impossible to the couple who partners with the Lord — absolutely nothing. You can change the atmosphere around you and wreak total havoc on the enemy's camp when your will lines up with God's will. You are a formidable team when this happens, and the enemy knows it.

Let me tell you something else. These decisions you and your spouse are making today with your visions will affect the generations that come after you. Your decisions don't just affect your immediate family and your children.

There are other people waiting for you on the other side of your obedience to God with your vision!

Think of all the other visionaries in the Bible: David, Solomon, Abraham, Esther, Ruth, Paul and John, just to name a few. Every decision these people made affected generations after them and whole nations.

You must understand that you are destined for greatness! Your decisions for your vision must take this fact into account. See yourself as the Lord does. Get a picture from Him of who He's really made you to be as individuals and then jointly as a couple. It's powerful stuff.

Are you stirred by this truth? I sincerely hope so! I believe that every single or couple who reads this book will be so radically changed that you will never go back to the way you were before. Be challenged! Step out of your place of comfort and partner with Jesus for an X-treme dream journey. You have been given the authority to become X-tremists in Jesus and impact the world with specific intent or divine purpose and vision that causes you to shake the world around you and change history.

We are told in 2 Timothy 3 and 4 what we as believers can expect to find in these end-time days. Today there is such a sense of desperation in the world, and yet the Lord says we can be at peace in Him. Standing firm on the wisdom He's given us in His word will keep us focused on the road before us. Vision and purpose keeps your feet from stumbling and your eyes focused on Him.

Here are seven tips for couples who want to live as X-tremists in God, who want to become a wonder couple:

X-Treme Wisdom for Wonder Couples

1. **Keep Jesus Christ in the center of your marriage.**

2. **When conflicts arise, and they will, take them to the Lord first in prayer.** Pray for your spouse all the time. This is your battle position folks. Never let the sun go down on your anger (Ephesians 4:26-27).

3. **Stay in the Word daily.** Renew your mind constantly. See things that are not as though they are (Ephesians 4:22- 23).

4. **Get an A-Team.** Let them cover you, as you cover them, with prayer. Make no vision decisions without the Lord's blessing and the blessing of your team. Many advisors make victory sure (Proverbs 11:14).

5. **Look for sweet, loving ways to encourage each other in your individual dreams.** Practice random acts of love and kindness with each other.

6. **Take time to celebrate large and small victories in your family.** Cheer each other on! In this way, you are constantly celebrating God's work in your life. Praise Him continually (Psalm 150:6).

7. **Complete your Vision Grids individually AND as a couple.** Live out your X-treme dreams as a lifestyle. Take the first step and make

changes as you go. Be honest with each other as you commit to do these things. Then stand back and watch God move on your behalf.

2 Timothy 2:7

Think over these things I am saying [understand them and grasp their application], for the Lord will grant you full insight and understanding in everything.

Dear couples, I fully believe that the Lord will meet you and your spouse right where you are in the X-treme dream process. Remember not to compare yourselves to anyone. What God has done for the others you've read about, He can do for you. He doesn't play favorites (Acts 10:34). It is not our Lord's nature to be this way.

Nothing is impossible with Him. So put your hands in His and get ready for the most exciting adventure ever. No one can live out this adventure like you can because it's just for you and your spouse. Sound amazing? It is! God promises us so much!

1 Corinthians 2:9

But as it is written, eye hath not seen, nor ear heard, neither have entered into the heart of man, the things which God hath prepared for them that love Him.

The last chapter will tell you how to proceed once you reach your X-treme dream.

God sees you doing it and so do I!

Chapter 11

X-tremist Living: What to do After you Suceed

Unless the distant goals of meaning, greatness and destiny are addressed,
we can't make an intelligent decision about what to do tomorrow morning
— much less set the long-term strategy for [our lives].
Nothing is more practical than for people to deepen themselves.
— Peter Koestenbaum

Most people will look back and realize they did not have a great life,
because it's just so easy to settle for a good life.
— Jim Collins

The greater danger for most of us lies not in setting our aim too high
and falling short; but in setting our aim too low, and achieving our mark.
— Michelangelo

Every human being possesses all 88 keys on the piano,
but most of us restrict our melodies to the middle octave.
— Deb Gottesman & Buzz Mauro

When I stand before God at the end of my life,
I would hope that I would not have a single bit of talent left,
and could say, "I used everything You gave me."
— Erma Bombeck

Our world is hungry for genuinely changed people.
— Richard J. Foster

I shared with you all the facets God has shared with me on the X-treme dream and how we can live out our vision as a lifestyle. Before I leave you to start your journey, I'd like to note a few more things about what to do once you succeed.

Whenever I do a vision seminar for an individual, couple or group, someone always asks if the Lord has completed everything He and I plotted out on my Vision Grid. My response is always, "Yes, and then some!"

You see, dear reader, I am now on my fourth grid. The Lord has completed and caused to come into my reality several dreams and milestones over the last six years.

What do you think that means for you? You are to keep right on X-treme dreaming when you reach success with the goals you have on your grid. This means that, as soon as you see the Lord bringing into completion those things in all three areas of your grid, it's time to draw up another grid or the next part of your X-treme dream.

This is so exciting to me, fellow visionaries, because this is how the Lord will keep revealing His fathomless nature to you! Scripture tells us that we have no idea all the things He keeps ready for us to receive. There is such an abundance of blessings stored up for us! You may feel finite, and you are, but remember that you become infinite when you partner with the Lord on your vision.

1 Corinthians 2:16

For who has known or understood the mind [the counsels and purposes] of the Lord so as to guide and instruct Him and give Him knowledge? But we have the Mind of Christ [the Messiah] and do hold the thoughts [feelings and purposes] of His heart.

The Lord wants you to keep right on going with Him as your vision's goals become a reality. As you achieve each part of your dream, ask Him what step you are to take next.

When I was in my mid-twenties, I began to set my sights on a position at the White House. I wrote one letter and found myself at the White House Staff Christmas Party. Within a week, I was invited to be a guest press secretary in the Vice President's office. When you use your gifts for His purposes, He brings you before great men (Proverbs 18:16). That year, I handled two White House assignments, and it was quite exciting. But when I got home to Denver, I found myself asking, "What's next, Lord?"

I heard that still, small voice tell me to prepare to go see Oprah Winfrey and present her with some special gifts. With God, one thing is always a building block or stepping stone to something greater.

My White House assignment and other special assignments while in government service were no big deal in and of themselves. God gave me those "tests" to prepare me for evangelistic trips to Chicago, Hollywood, Nashville and other places around the globe. He said to my spirit that if I could be trusted to hear and obey Him amid the noise in Washington, DC, then He could trust me with Oprah and many others.

Shaunya and I did go and meet Oprah a couple of days after her birthday and gave her what the Lord put on our hearts to share with her. Once again, He made a way where there seemed to be none.

We traveled by train to the Windy City and thoroughly enjoyed the leisurely ride. Once we got to Chicago, the sights and sounds of famous Michigan Avenue greeted us, a smorgasbord for our senses. The next day, we caught a cab and went to Harpo Studios, home of the "Oprah Winfrey Show." Just stepping inside the door was exhilarating because we knew how difficult it was to get tickets to the world's #1 talk show. God had worked a miracle!

By the time taping began, I was already praying about what the Lord wanted me to do once the audience began to leave. I felt like He wanted us to be still and wait to be the last people in the studio. We did that, and ended up having a lovely conversation with Oprah about our reason for coming and our company vision. God even opened up the door for us to personally give her the birthday presents we brought with us from Denver! Mission Impossible became Mission Possible because the Lord was with us.

Once we were assured that we had done all God wanted us to do, we left to celebrate on Michigan Avenue with a four-course lunch at the beautiful Escada Café.

This is another example of God's putting His super abilities on my natural self. That's a dangerous mixture when you're sent out by Him to do Kingdom business. No foe can withstand the favor of the Lord on His people. You, dear visionary, become unstoppable!

After the miraculous visit to see Oprah, I kept on dreaming with God. He said that I had passed the next test and should prepare for a trip to Hollywood to meet with top Hollywood producers and studio executives. I didn't know it then, but that trip to Hollywood would begin to link me with influential non-Christians in the film industry. All of the connections made then are solid relationships I enjoy now, sealed by the Lord.

This X-treme lifestyle will keep you on your toes, folks, and is anything but dull. You will find yourself in the Land of Signs and Wonders every day if you take the Lord at His word and never look back.

God has completed so many of my dreams to date. **I record every single one** and I make a point to celebrate these things with friends and family as often as they occur. You can, too!

What will happen at this stage of the game is a serious change in you and your life. You will see a new consistency like never before. Living as I've outlined in this book will become second nature to you. Your depth of intimacy with Jesus Christ will be so grounded that nothing but His will and purpose for your life will satisfy you. He will be the only One who can quench your thirst on the journey.

Signs and wonders will occur in rapid-fire fashion around and to you, because the presence of God will surround you like a shield (Psalm 5:12). People will be drawn to you because of the Christ that is so evident in you. Are you ready to become a people magnet?

Your expectancy will go up 100 % in the Lord. When He tells you to jot an idea down on your next Vision Grid, you will expect Him to perform whatever is necessary to attain that item, because He will have already shown Himself strong to you in so many ways. And you will see that your will lines up with His will for your life. This is what I mean by a change in lifestyle.

The joy of the Lord is your strength at this point, too. Why? Because you bring joy to Him when you tell others over and over again how He's made you victorious. Rehearsing your victories in Him brings Him joy and causes Him to shower you with amazing strength to accomplish all He has for you.

Increase in every area of your life will come at this point in an exponential way. God's nature is to multiply over and over what you and I give to Him. You will see it in every area of your life in such a way that you won't be able to contain it all. It will become yet another testimony of God's hand in your life.

Do you see why your vision is so important? Each of us is spiritually activated to set into motion God's plan of authority on this earth and for all eternity, when we will live and reign with Him. The purpose and vision He's designed for you are not just for now but for ever and ever (Revelation 20:4).

For now, remember to hold onto your partnership with Jesus and keep asking Him to show you the next part of your vision. The X-treme dream is not over until He says it's over, so keep on going. He is the Alpha and Omega (beginning and end), so it's His place to say when your vision has reached its end.

You might get bits and pieces of the next grid or part of your next dream before your first grid is a reality. When that happens, just make another grid and start storing up those pieces of the dream in those squares until you and the Lord can get to them. Again, keeping a pad of paper by your bed each night allows you to jot down your thoughts and ideas, then go right back to sleep. Your pad corrals your thoughts for you. Don't spend too much time wondering about how those things are going to come to pass. Just put them on the next grid for safekeeping until God opens the next door.

Be ready to add to or delete from the team you've built at this point as well. New levels of a dream or vision often require new kinds of strategy and advisors. There is wisdom and safety for us when we take the time to counsel with others. For this reason, you must keep an A-Team at all times. God has a season for everything and, as you mature in this process, you may sense a need for more people on your team or you may need to release someone who no longer fits. This is healthy for you to realize.

Your integrity and your accountability also increases when you do this. You can expect to be asked to be on an A-Team by someone else who is just beginning their vision journey. This is an honor, so enjoy it, but also remember the responsibility that comes with it. This is how the body of Christ helps us hold each other up.

Keep your patience in this season, because where the Lord has been quick for a season, He may also be slow for a season. The key is to remember that He is still on the throne and still has your best interests at heart (Jeremiah 29:11-13). Every day with the Lord is new. He thinks outside your grid. His ways are higher than ours, and yet He knows exactly what we need, and how and when we need it. Isn't that comforting to know? We must totally trust Him with our hearts and lives. Giving yourself in this way is the best gift you can offer Him.

Follow the process outlined in this book and live the X-treme dream life. The Word of God never changes, but the depth and breadth of your X-treme dreams will. No two of us are exactly alike. It's part of His plan. There is no big bang, because there is nothing about our lives that was formed by chance or accident.

Now that you've walked through the discovery process of your X-treme dream, are you ready to set out on the journey? You are going to have the time of your life. No day will ever be the same again. You won't be able to sleep sometimes because of all the joy and stirring in your spirit of things to come.

Just release yourself and your dreams to the Lord. He is Love and His love for you has no depth. That's right — it's fathomless (Romans

8:38-39). He will be your constant traveling companion because He promises to never leave or forsake you (Hebrews 13:5).

Take a moment to read this poem written by my friend, author and speaker, Linda Evans Shepherd. It's a great reminder that you are not your own and that we must give our dreams and visions to the Lord, our Savior and lover of our souls.

It's Your Turn, Lord
I found my dream and held it tight,
And prayed for wings to give it flight.
But yet it stayed earthbound with me,
Because I did not set it free.

Although I held it to my heart,
Somehow it seemed to fall apart.
"Oh, Lord," I cried unhappily.
"Why did you take my dream from me?"

"My child, your dream is incomplete,
Until you lay it at My feet.
Unless you give your dream to Me,
It cannot find its destiny."

I knew I had to let it go,
For I had nothing left to show,
Until my dream was in His hand,
I could not see His plan so grand.

At last I saw what He would do,
He shaped my broken dream anew.
For dreams will never find reward,
Until we say, "It's Your turn, Lord."

It has been my absolute pleasure to share my heart with you in this way! I devoutly want each of you to become ALL the Lord originally designed you to be. Cheering people on in the race to their personal finish lines is my deepest passion. And I am proud to boast about all that our Head Coach, Jesus Christ, has done in my life and the lives of so many others on the X-treme dream journey. Being on His coaching staff is such a joy and total kick! He has taught me the strategies for overcomers. I pray they bless you as much as they have me. Now get out there and be the ferocious threat to the enemy that God says you are!

About the Author

Charlynne Boddie is a professional journalist, TV producer and media consultant/trainer, with over 15 years experience in print and broadcast media, all levels of government, academia and the entertainment industry. She has produced and been featured in several award-winning TV productions. In addition, she has served as press officer for two White House assignments and is a former federal spokesperson for several of America's largest natural disasters.

Ms. Boddie is a well-traveled evangelist to foreign nations and feels called to minister to movers and shakers at every level of the TV, film and music industries. Charlynne is also a former president of the international professional organization *Women in Film, Video and Television*, which is headquartered in Los Angeles, California.

In 1988, she received an honors degree in television production from Oral Roberts University (ORU) in Tulsa, Oklahoma. While attending ORU, she wrote her first successful TV pilot and worked as a drive-time newscaster for a local Tulsa radio station.

Charlynne's desire to work among her Christian and non-Christian colleagues in the TV and film industry caused her to create Denver-based ColorBlind Productions with her screenwriting sister Shaunya. ColorBlind Productions is a development house for theatrical, TV, film and music productions. It is not only a business but also a ministry for professionals throughout the industry in America and overseas.

Together, the sisters are the hosts and founders of *The Entertainment Summit* (a one-on-one ministry weekend in the Colorado Rockies) to edify and encourage Christians in entertainment, from Hollywood to New York and Europe. Many professionals have been blessed on a personal level and changed at these intimate weekends.

Charlynne and Shaunya are the recipients of a 2000 Telly Award for an original TV pilot called *Reel Sisters*. The *Reel Sisters* concept was picked up by the LeSEA Broadcasting Network in South Bend, Indiana, in November 2002. The Reel Sisters movie review segment is seen in 135 US markets and has an audience of 312 million viewers worldwide on cable and satellite.

Charlynne is also a licensed minister at New Beginnings Worship Center in Aurora, Colorado, which is under the leadership of Pastors Lewis and Ramona Brown.

Future aspirations for Charlynne include a deep desire to continue traveling overseas to equip the saints, spread the gospel of Jesus Christ, and purchase a ranch in Colorado that would serve to meet special ministry needs of Christians and movers and shakers around the globe. Charlynne is single and resides in Aurora, Colorado, with her sister and a Schnauzer named Reilly.

Contact Information:
Charlynne M. Boddie
P.O. Box 12127
Aurora, CO 80012
303-692-7770
blwheeler01@hotmail.com